Before she Knew JESUS

A Devotional: The Raw and Refining Stories
of a Woman's Road to Redemption

Before She Knew JESUS

Forward by Jessica Shakir

TAMRA ANDRESS

F.I.T. in Faith LLC
Virginia Beach, Virginia
Fitinfaithpress.com
Editing: Sharon Miles Frese

Library of Congress Control Number: 2025900812

ISBN: 978-1-7379022-6-3

The moral right of Tamra Andress as the primary author of this work and founder of F.I.T. Press has been asserted by her in accordance with the Copyrights, Designs and Patents Act of 1988.

Scripture quotations marked (CSB) are been taken from the Christian Standard Bible®, Copyright © 2017 by Holman Bible Publishers. Used by permission. Christian Standard Bible•, and CSB® are federally registered trademarks of Holman Bible Publishers.

Scripture quotations marked (KJV) are taken from the KING JAMES VERSION, public domain.

Scripture quotations marked (ESV) are taken from THE HOLY BIBLE, ENGLISH STANDARD VERSION®, Copyright© 2001 by Crossway, a publishing ministry of Good News Publishers. Used by permission.

Scripture quotations marked (NIV) are taken from THE HOLY BIBLE, NEW INTERNATIONAL VERSION®. Copyright© 1973, 1978, 1984, 2011 by Biblica, Inc.™. Used by permission of Zondervan

Scripture quotations marked (NKJV) are taken from the NEW KING JAMES VERSION®. Copyright© 1982 by Thomas Nelson, Inc. Used by permission. All rights reserved.

Scripture quotations marked (NLT) are taken from the Holy Bible, New Living Translation, copyright ©1996, 2004, 2015 by Tyndale House Foundation. Used by permission of Tyndale House Publishers, Carol Stream, Illinois 60188. All rights reserved.

Scripture quotations marked (MSG) are taken from *THE MESSAGE*. Copyright © 1993, 1994, 1995, 1996, 2000, 2001, 2002. Used by permission of NavPress Publishing Group.

Scripture quotations marked (Amp) are taken from the AMPLIFIED® BIBLE, Copyright© 1954, 1958, 1962, 1964, 1965, 1987 by the Lockman Foundation Used by Permission. (www.Lockman.org).

Scripture quotations marked (TPT) are from The Passion Translation®. Copyright © 2017, 2018, 2020 by Passion & Fire Ministries, Inc. Used by permission. All rights reserved. ThePassionTranslation.com.

Scripture quotations marked (RGT) are from The Revised Geneva Translation (RGT), an easy-to-understand modernization of the 1599 Geneva Bible. More information at https://5talentsaudio.com/.

THIS BOOK IS DEDICATED TO . . .

. . . the biological and spiritual daughters of each of the authors, whose stories fill these pages. We want you to know there is a committed papa, a close friend, a guide, a teacher, and a great counselor.
There's a protector and provider, a lover and a healer.
There is a God who loves you and delights in you. And even before you feel seen, known, and loved, He sees, knows, and loves you fiercely. We hope this book draws you into intimacy in a way you've never known and calls you into spiritual maturity so you can
live a life of fulfillment and abundant fruit. And ultimately,
you can then turn around to more of God's girls and point them to their maker. Say yes to sanctification. The refiner's fire is worth it.

Table of Contents

Foreword: By Jessica Shakir ix
Introduction: By Tamra Andress... 1

Chapter 1 Freedom in Obedience 9
  By Victoria Ciresi

Chapter 2 My Undivided Heart 21
  By Jenny Ingels

Chapter 3 When Forgiveness Feels Offensive 33
  By Jennifer Beeman

Chapter 4 Shame Is No Longer My Name 43
  By Kali Dunson

Chapter 5 Sandcastles 57
  By Rebekah (Becky) Vasquez

Chapter 6 The Mess of the Making 67
  By Tamra Andress

Chapter 7 Becoming His Disciple.. 79
  By Jori O'Neale

Chapter 8 The Invitation for More 89
  By Ashley Weston

Chapter 9 The Journey to Trust Jesus for Our Loved Ones........ 99
  By April Foster

Chapter 10 A New Name 111
  By Amber Love

Chapter 11 Living in the Truth of His Love................................... 123
  By Christina Blincoe

Chapter 12 Going Through the Motions 137
By Heather Demorest

Chapter 13 Embracing the Unknown 149
By Kess Scharff

Chapter 14 His Plan, His Timing, and Her Willing Heart..........163
By Teresa Holbrooks Nichols

Chapter 15 Awakening to Truth: Choosing the Narrow Path
over Deception..179
By Candice Brown

Appendix...189
Acknowledgments..193
Supporting Resources for Women...194

FOREWORD
By Jessica Shakir

I've always been enamored with the word *before*. Like an empty stage awaiting its first scene or an open road that holds the promise of something new, it whispers to my creative soul, "Transformation is coming." Filled with curiosity, I wonder: *What beauty lies just ahead? What story will God reveal?* The "before" naturally awakens my anticipation for the "after."

Words are an obsession Tamra and I both share. We've spent hours marveling at their power to woo hearts and shift atmospheres. Our imaginations run wild as we revel in the truth that God's instrument of choice when crafting the cosmos was *words*. I love how joyous contemplation has connected our hearts. Much like Mary and Elizabeth, our sisterhood has stirred something God-entrusted within us.

If you know Tamra, you've seen how her brilliance and honesty create both a refuge and a canvas where others can explore their divine potential, refine their message, and step boldly into the calling God has placed on their lives. Her gift for bringing people—and words—together is nothing short of breathtaking, as you will soon experience.

Sitting at the feet of Jesus has completely changed my life, and so it is with deep humility and fervor that I pen this foreword for *Before She Knew Jesus*. These words are more than just ink on a page—they reflect my life's work: helping women explore the beauty of God as we deepen our knowledge of His Word—together! What a celebratory way to link arms with my sisters, sharing stories of rescue and redemption that unveil the greatest adventure of all—to know and be known by the living God.

Adventurous: Would you use this word to describe your relationship with Jesus? Does *intimate* speak truth about your spiritual life? Would you dare call it *sensuous*?

Step outside and gaze at the stars. Let the vastness of the heavens stir wonder in your heart as you contemplate the eternality of our triune God. Can this be done through logic alone? Or does it demand all your senses to truly behold His glory? (And yes, that's what *sensuous* means—just in case you were nervous!) Psalm 34:8 (CSB) invites us to "Taste and see that the Lord is good." Both the Old and New Testaments command us to love the Lord our God with all our *heart, soul, strength* . . . and *mind*, and 2 Corinthians 2:14 reveals that God spreads "the aroma of the knowledge of him" through us.

To pursue the knowledge of God, we must engage our entire being; to truly love Him requires the same full-bodied surrender. It's an intimate act that demands our full participation. *To know Him is to love Him.* How true this is of our Savior—a marriage of knowing and loving, a union of mind and heart, a melding of Heaven and Earth. We must also remember that knowing requires being known, and loving requires being loved. Otherwise, we're just reading about the ocean instead of jumping right in.

In the biblical sense, *knowing* is synonymous with *intimacy*. Genesis 4:1 (KJV) says, "Adam knew Eve his wife; and she conceived." The Hebrew word here is *yāḏaʿ* (Strong's Concordance H3045), meaning "to know by experience"— not just with data.

Similarly, in John 17:3 (ESV), when Jesus said, "And this is eternal life, that they know you, the only true God, and Jesus Christ whom you have sent," the Greek word *ginōskō* (G1097) also points to experiential knowledge—not just intellectual insight.

My entire spiritual life has been a journey from having knowledge *about* Jesus to being intimately wrapped up in the ravishing reality *of* Jesus. Moment by moment, I'm learning to swim further out into His ocean of grace. While I have a lifetime of testimonies, my earliest memory of being rescued comes to mind.

Foreword

When I was four, our sweet daddy died, and our mama became a widow in an instant. My siblings and I were left utterly shocked. I'm told I didn't speak for weeks. While I don't remember that part, I do recall being in our yard, looking up at the sky and thinking, *God, you took my daddy. . . . I need you to be my daddy now.* How does a child even think those thoughts? I'm not entirely sure, but I do know God met me in that sorrow in such a real way, and ever since, I've lived with the reality of eternity in my heart and the warmth of heaven on my skin.

Experience: That's what transforms us. It's walking through the valley of the shadow of death, coming out the other side, and realizing there was only one set of footprints all along. It's being carried by the very arms of God and protected by the compassion of His heart—not just observing it but *living* it. That's what sets a soul on fire.

In *Before She Knew Jesus*, it's not the "before" that gets the spotlight—it's **Jesus**. He's the catalyst for every conversion revealed in the chapters ahead. He's the Light of the World who illuminates our every shadow. He's the Redeemer of souls and stories, and He longs to be known by you for all eternity.

He proved it by paving the very road to redemption with His own blood. The cosmic King, wrapped in human skin, became the sacrificial Lamb who took away the sins of the world. With the agony of the curse penetrating His body and the loneliness of the cross surrounding Him, Jesus felt the cost of love. Yes, love drove Him to finish the work of redemption through His crucifixion—and resurrection!

It is this same intimate love that fuels every woman's testimony in this devotional. My prayer is that wherever you are in your spiritual journey, you allow the redeeming blood of Jesus to wash over you and take you deeper into the majestic waters of His goodness. May the joy of knowing Jesus transform the way you love, and may His beauty shine through your life as a beacon of hope for a weary world.

JESSICA SHAKIR has been a student of beauty all her life. With twenty-five years as a Celebrity Hair & Makeup Artist, TV Beauty Expert, and Creative Director, Jessica has a unique ability to create moments that spark wonder. Over the past few years, her love for all things lovely has blossomed into a deep exploration of theological aesthetics—the sacred intersection of beauty and the divine. In the stillness of her studies, she was drawn to one powerful question: *Can one truly study beauty without encountering the Creator?* And in answering, she found herself captivated by a much grander vision of Beauty.

In essence, Jessica has been a student of the Living God all her life, captivated by His Goodness, Truth, and Beauty. She shares this passion through speaking, preaching, and writing, as well as facilitating theological studies and conversations, hosting Eden Retreats across the nation, leading Abide Book Club and Prayer Club, hosting the annual *Advent Celebration Series*, co-hosting the *Girls Gone Holy* podcast, and offering Co-Create, a spiritual formation coaching experience for creative kingdom women worldwide.

As the founder of The Beautiful Mind Academy, Jessica leads a global community of Jesus-loving women, spanning thirty-three nations, guiding them to reflect God's glory through creativity. She loves connecting with people from diverse cultures, learning new languages, celebrating life with wild abandon, and marveling at the God of Wonders, together!

Foreword

With a degree in visual communications and decades of experience in visual storytelling, Jessica also helps clients craft impactful, God-glorifying brands that capture hearts and minds. She believes, as redeemed creations in Christ, we should be the most creative, joyous souls on Earth.

Jessica and her beloved husband Vincent are embracing life in Sweet Home Alabama, restoring their first home, dreaming and co-creating together, and eagerly anticipating what God has in store for their next chapter.

INTRODUCTION
by Tamra Andress

This book is for the hungry, for the soul longing for fresh wind and deep adventure, and for the one who craves to be known but often finds herself void of being seen. This is written for the woman ready to rid herself of the shallow life and uncover the depths of who she is created to be while discovering how much her Creator adores her. This book is for the gal facing a fire, perhaps stuck at a crossroads of her faith, crying out for something more. You are not alone. You are not crazy. You are not worthless. And you are surely purposed to be reading this book for such a time as this.

You must be forewarned. Two things are probable. Either I'm about to ruffle your feathers and cause your fight-or-flight system to respond with the crossing of your arms or furrowing of your brow, or, as I hope, you'll grab your trumpet and lean in next to the incredible daughters of the King writing this book to amplify what the Lord is doing in and through His women at-large in this era. Regardless of which side of the pendulum you're on, I need us to get on the same page. First, you must know we are with you and for you, no matter where we find you. Second, you must understand that this book's very heartbeat was ignited to bring everyone into the conversation, with an invitation to explore a rich intimacy while practicing the war cry of dwelling daughters. But don't let the word *everyone* or this idea of *belonging* be skewed. While we are surely developing a safe place to explore, we are not afraid to draw a line in the sand in Truth and Love. After all, Jesus came to divide with a sword (Matthew 10:34, NIV).

So let's take a few deep breaths together—slowly in through your nose, holding at the top for three seconds, and releasing at the same pace. And again—no, really. I'm asking you to pause the scroll and refrain from jumping to the next paragraph or chapter. These actions reset the parasympathetic nervous system and stimulate the part of the brain that controls your emotions and focus so you can be most attentive to what the Holy Spirit wants to reveal in these words. I encourage you to return to this practice as you read through this book, not only to center yourself but to receive.

Breath. This is a precious blessing we so often take for granted, and yet, in the journey of seeking and knowing Him more, He reminds us to slow down and breathe. On Mount Sinai, in the book of Exodus, God revealed His very nature in His name as a reminder of our inhale (YH) and our exhale (WH). Moses was the first to hear Him say His name, YHWY (commonly spelled *Yahweh*), which means "I AM." Some believe the Hebrew letters used in His name literally mean "arm, behold, nail, behold." Umm, hello, how can you not see Jesus in the Old Testament or not see the triune God in the depths of His very spoken Word? How rich was Moses's knowing of Him at that moment?

When we pause, we can more easily reflect on the intricacies of His being rather than the world's depiction that has been simply minimized to the cross. I say that with a full understanding of the offense those two words, *simply minimized*, could cause. Nothing about the greatest sacrifice of our Father through His Son is simple. But we see the cross tattooed on people's bodies and displayed around their necks. We see it on street corners and steeples, yet the minimized weight and the lack of fear and reverence have left us fashioned to a pace that ignores breath but relishes in empty words and actions. If you're wearing a cross, then you must be a real Christian, right? Ultimately, if we stay at the cross, we forget that the crucifixion sacrifice alone doesn't fully represent His gift. Without the tomb *and* resurrection, we wouldn't have eternal salvation. This is the Gospel, after all.

Anthony Hart, one of my dear brothers in Christ and fellow pastors with The Founder Collective (our nonprofit, dedicated to marketplace ministry: www.thefoundercollective.org), says it best. "The church has been stuck at the cross for far too long, lacking the power of the resurrection and leaving us weak and fearful of the world, still answering to our own insecurities. Jesus intended for that moment to create a movement to follow Him, not to stay in the shadow of our sins."

Introduction

These days, the foot of the cross looks like Disney World. And that's where we stay—popularized and glamorized while forgetting the purity and purpose. We are consumed by the hot-topic buzzwords and slogans (just a sinner saved by grace, faith > fear, or not today, Satan) that permeate the "Christianese" language and have further cemented a lackluster culture. In fact, it's so dried up that even non-Christians are adopting the sayings and turning a profit from His Word while we sit idly by with our iced lattes and Bible T-shirts, allowing it to happen. Is this the depth of our love on display? Is this the richness of our faith and salvation expressed for all the world to see? Is this the extent of our follow-up to the command, "Go and tell," given to us in Mark 16:15?

The use of this silly, extracted language that omits the depths of who He is and who we are to Him is like adopting pig Latin back in the day so our parents wouldn't understand what we and our friends were talking about. The problem is, it's the antithesis of Jesus's ministry, which was meant to be plain and simple. You see, the religious Sadducees and Pharisees already tried the shtick of confusion, with educated language and rules to weigh every word and decision. And though power still seemed to be on their side, true heavenly power and authority were restricted, and their manipulative initiatives didn't serve them personally or corporately when it came to intimacy with God.

I think of the story of Nicodemus and the eager moments of hopefulness where he explored something more: the warmth of affection, the depths of wisdom, the unending love, and the deep sense of knowing. Research couldn't pinpoint it. Religious practices couldn't secure it, and no one was proclaiming it—at least not those he deemed "honorable" because, surely, John the Baptist had already made a holy ruckus.

How many different types of modern-day Nicodemuses exist?

Those on the fringe
Those who have a past

Those who are encamped with the other army
Those raised in the rules and regulations of the Church
Those who are told to keep quiet
Those who are wildly educated
Those who have been coached into the worldly belief system
Those who find solace in a controlled community that holds them hostage
Those who have an eager spirit but a weak soul
Those who carry their labels as a badge of honor
Those who self-seek rather than surrender

Here we are in the chasm. This place where many of us get stuck is filled with invitations to become like everyone else: to act a certain way, to flow a certain way, and to practice a certain way, all while "The Way" is as close as our breath and as clear as a clean conscience. Here's the variable. He *is* "the way and the truth and the life" (John 14:6, NIV), but what we've settled for is their way, their truth, and their life.

Unfortunately, the latter scenario is much more prevalent, even in the lives of "Christians." You've sat in the pews and at tables. You've been to the events. You've attended services and confessions. I can give the benefit of the doubt and believe all of those activities were intended to get to know the "All-Knowing," but without humility or effective discipleship, it becomes another systematic exchange of time, money, and to-dos. Ultimately, through a lack of intimacy with others, a surface relationship with Christ, and a skewed sense of authority, you're experiencing the same religiosity that Jesus himself rejected. Now it's just packaged in the four walls of a trendy, wood-paneled building with a coffee shop, fueling our desire to *be* "good and alive"—insert caffeine.

Okay, okay, I know this all sounds a bit depressing and perhaps too big of a blanket to throw over all of what's happening in the Western Church (because there are certainly beautiful treasure troves, transformations, and reformations happening that you'll learn about here too). But let's not stop short of the curiosity that's been tickled. Otherwise, you, too, can consider

Introduction

yourself a Nicodemus. You must recall that not all the traps the enemy sets appear to be evil or harmful. Consider his first temptation: a piece of fruit. It's healthy, isn't it? But isn't it ironic that, over time, food has become one of the biggest contributors to death in America? You see, his conniving ways always start with a seemingly wholesome presentation, tickling our appetite for what appears to be good. Meanwhile, pebble by pebble and brick by brick, Satan turns what seems to be a support into a stronghold.

We can't stay in this chasm any longer. The earth is shaking, groaning, and craving for a revolution of not just seekers but knowers!

Time and time again, the Word tells us to wake up! Wake up to the lies. Wake up to the control. Wake up to the manipulation. Wake up to fear-mongering. And, ultimately, start anew. But we've gotten so complacent and apathetic, avoiding any real change—let alone conviction. And if we feel any sense of discomfort, we crawl back to our blanket zones and even our shackles.

The age-old story of "The Elephant Rope" comes to mind. You see, elephants are obviously capable of uprooting trees with their trunks. They are strong beyond our comprehension. And yet, the baby elephant, who is first tied to a tree trunk, doesn't quite have the strength to yank the trunk or break the rope. So, after several attempts as a young calf, it ceases to try. And even though it is eventually strong enough to break the rope, it believes it cannot and never tries to break free again—hopeless and conditioned to believe that "This is all there is to life; I'll be stuck here forever."

Have you ever thought the same way about your relationship with Jesus or this Christian walk? Perhaps, in some ways, you've felt tethered. This book is here to loose you! *To call you into your true design, dominion, and destiny, all while you delight in your divine nature and Maker.*

> *To call you into your true design, dominion, and destination, all while you delight in your divine nature and Maker.*

The heart of this book is to address the experience of sanctification, which, by definition, is the action or process of making something holy, free from sin, or purified. It can also be the act of making something appear morally right or acceptable. But depending on your history or level of understanding, I know that the word *sanctification* can leave the tongue with a bitter taste. So my coauthors and I have chosen to take a different path to the same end. Like my first memoir, *Always Becoming: sex, shame, and Love*, this is a book about becoming like Jesus, getting to know Him and all the many roles He plays in our lives, emulating His good nature, adopting His will, and welcoming the sweetest bounty of being known by Him—being set apart and sanctified.

This collection of stories will challenge you, convict you, remake and shape you, but, ultimately, it will invite you—***deeper***. These aren't our pre-Jesus, post-Jesus stories. They are the walking-it-out, imperfect-holiness experiences, learned lessons, and intimate moments where He made himself known. *Before She Knew Jesus*, like, really knew Him, she was a Nicodemus, a Saul, a Jacob. The wrestling in the shadows brought us to His glorious light and gave us a new name: His daughter. Chosen. Set apart. Known.

Before I knew Jesus . . . I was lukewarm. This book is your fire starter. Get ready to be set ablaze for Christ.

Through sanctification, the surrendering of our lives to Christ, we are accepted, made right in God's eyes, and no longer apart from Him—we are set apart.

Victoria Ciresi

Chapter 1

Freedom in Obedience
By Victoria Ciresi

While we are living in sin, we are **apart** from God, separated. Through *sanctification*, the surrendering of our lives to Christ, we are accepted, made right in God's eyes, and no longer apart from Him—we are **set apart**. We become seen, holy, and clean, and it's through this process that we can truly lean into being set apart and living His purpose for our lives.

MY ENCOUNTER

Have you ever had a secret, something known by very few people or maybe no one at all, something that you believed was ugly and dark and had the power to tear your world apart, something that would wake you up at night, gnaw at the pit of your stomach, and rob you of your peace, your joy, and your harmony? Going into my twenties, I carried a secret deep inside that I believed would need to stay there forever.

THAT WAS BEFORE I KNEW JESUS

It was a rainy Friday night after a long week of exams and extra hours put in at work. My roommate and I wanted to unwind and decided to reward ourselves for surviving another grueling week. We popped open some wine, got the tequila ready, and called some friends to hang out. This had become a typical way to kick off our weekends—Friday night house party, Saturday morning hangover, and veg out all day, only getting up to eat (which usually involved something greasy, comforting, or my favorite: Italian).

This Friday evening was different for me. Something had been stirring all week. I felt restless. I tangibly remember a nagging feeling that I couldn't quite pinpoint, a longing in my heart that felt like an ache, and a nervousness in my gut that tightened like a knot. The weather was gray, and temperatures were cool. It had rained off and on for almost the entire week. I found myself unable to enjoy the party and was completely overwhelmed by the hum of conversation, the thumping of music in the background, and the feelings within. I needed peace, calm, clarity, and ease, but the party was just causing more unrest . . . so I left.

I didn't know where to go, but I knew I needed to get away. Before I realized it, I was pulling into the parking lot of the building where I worked. I wanted to go somewhere to be alone—somewhere to just sit, be still, and think. As I entered the parking lot, a place I had pulled into almost every day for the last year, there in front of me was a tree I had never "seen" before. Staring through the windshield, the headlights magnifying the drops of rain pouring down, I noticed this tree for the very first time. It was shaped like a cross.

THIS IS WHERE I MET JESUS

The nagging feeling that had plagued me all week compelled me to get out of the car. The longing in my heart that felt like an ache drew me toward the cross. The nervousness in my gut that felt like a knot brought me to my knees. I found myself completely surrendered at the foot of the cross! Tears streamed down my cheeks as rain poured over me. What felt like minutes turned into hours. There was stillness in the moment, but my sensations were electrified. There was such an awareness of each one of my previously unmet needs. It was an experience that words can't fully capture the depths of.

On that night at the cross, where I met Jesus, I surrendered the dark and unbearable secret from my past, a secret that I could no longer carry—I'd had an abortion.

Before that encounter, I believed I was a Christian. I believed God existed. I grew up in church. I prayed sometimes. But it wasn't until that night that I truly **saw** the cross and understood what it meant to let go. It was at that moment that my relationship with Jesus began. It was at that moment that I realized the gravity of my need and the truth in what it meant to surrender my life to Him. In my brokenness and pain, carrying the weight of this sin, He met me there. . . . I was the woman at the well.

MY SOUL WAS THIRSTY

In Chapter Four of the Book of John, a Samaritan woman comes to the well where Jesus is sitting. She chose to come at a time when no one else would likely be there. Burdened by a life of sin and seeking fulfillment in relationships, she carried shame and hid the depths of her secrets, which led to her isolation. Jesus engages her by asking for a drink of water. He is fully aware of her history and speaks to her without judgment. The night I met Jesus, I, too, carried feelings of isolation and unworthiness caused by guilt and shame from my past mistakes. I felt a longing to be understood and accepted.

Until that moment, my heart was heavy; my soul was thirsty, and I felt broken as if I could shatter into pieces at any moment. I tried to be the girl who could hold it all together—and may have appeared as such outwardly—but the internal struggles I faced were destroying me more and more each day. I could not even speak the word *abortion* without trembling. I suppressed any memory or emotion that would bubble up and worked hard to forget the past, anesthetizing myself with friends, parties, alcohol, food, and the busyness of life.

Like the Samaritan woman who went to the well at an unusual time of day, I would avoid certain conversations and people for fear of being judged. I lived in shame and isolated myself emotionally, feeling that my flaws and the dark secret of my past would disqualify me from ever receiving their full acceptance. This fear of judgment led me to withdraw from meaningful relationships and opportunities for connection, perpetuating a cycle of loneliness and guilt. The further I ran from it, the harder my heart became.

Jesus's interaction with the Samaritan woman at the well and with me that night at the cross proves that He meets each of us where we are. He acknowledges our past but focuses on offering us freedom—"living water." In John 4:14 (NLT), Jesus tells the woman, "But those who drink the water I give will never be thirsty again. It becomes a fresh, bubbling spring within them, giving them eternal life." The living water He offers provides freedom from shame. We can have true healing not by avoiding or hiding from our past but by confronting it with grace and receiving His love and forgiveness. Jesus did not condemn the Samaritan woman or me. Instead, He revealed that shame does not define our worth, and redemption and transformation are always possible, no matter the weight of what we carry.

> ...shame does not define our worth, and redemption and transformation are always possible, no matter the weight of what we carry.

God had been working on me for some time, and I was able to see how He orchestrated each step leading to this "at the cross" moment where I surrendered my secret. I think back on that evening and realize that, for over a year, every time I pulled into that parking lot, the tree had always been there. What I saw then and continue to see in my journey of faith is that God's timing is always perfect, and if we look for Him, He is guiding our steps. He is always there. In Proverbs 16:9 (NLT), it is written, "We can make our plans, but the LORD determines our steps." A week after my "at the cross" moment, that tree was gone. It had been removed by the building landscape company because it was dying. If that moment had been just one week later, I would have never seen that "cross." God had framed my encounter at just the right time and orchestrated each step.

When you meet Jesus and accept what He is offering, it is the most *amazing*, *wonderful*, and *freeing* feeling in the whole world. Like the woman at the well who moved from living in shame to living with boldness, the thirst in my soul became quenched, and an inner light was ignited. The hardened heart I was carrying softened, and a sense of freedom was birthed inside me. I couldn't get enough of God's Word, and with the courage only He could provide, I became a witness for Him, just like the woman at the well.

Surrendering our lives to Jesus does not mean all our problems will go away. In John 16:33 (NLT), Jesus says, "I have told you all this so that you may have peace in me. Here on earth you will have many trials and sorrows." The beauty of knowing Jesus is the promise of hope that He gives us, a hope that transcends our current circumstances and sustains us through the darkest moments, allowing peace, comfort, and rest. Jesus continues in verse 33, "But take heart, because I have overcome the world." In our journey of sanctification, we need to let Jesus be our hope and guide, especially when the world gets heavy.

I LOST MY WAY

In my middle to late thirties, I found that I was losing my way. I lost sight of my identity, allowing the wrong things to guide me and the world's voice to creep in. In the book *More Than Enough: The Silent Struggle of a Woman's Identity*, I wrote that what motivated me during this season, how I prioritized my life, and who I sought counsel from became misaligned. Yes, I knew Jesus, but I wasn't focusing on our relationship or placing it first and above everything else. So when the world started shutting down because of COVID-19, I let fear seep in, and my human nature tried to carry the load alone. Even though I had repented of the sins I committed in the past, forgiven those who had hurt me, and made the decision to realign my life to be Christ-centered, I was no longer living that way. I was no longer fully surrendered to Him and tried to control everything around me.

Hebrews 10:36 (NLT) shares that "Patient endurance is what you need now, so that you will continue to do God's will. Then you will receive all that he has promised." I began doing my will and, oh, how far I fell. There was no true fruit in my life. My roles as a wife and a mother were put on the back burner as I focused on my selfish desires to guide others through a pandemic and find purpose in my role as a business leader. I put almost all my energy into my job and sought validation for my work performance based on the standards of others. I prioritized the relationships with my colleagues and the strength of our business over my loved ones and the strength of my family. I found myself making poor decisions and, ultimately, descended into deep despair to the point of completely losing my way and fearing for my marriage.

THE LORD NEVER LEFT MY SIDE

Jesus desires to walk alongside us in each step of our journey. He will carry our burdens if we only ask. In that new season of despair, I found myself on the side of a bed in a hotel room, feeling completely empty and unworthy despite being saved. I cried out, and, wow, did He speak. He reminded me that He never left my side, that He loves me, and that my sins are forgiven. I just needed to trust Him and be obedient to His asks, and He would fight the battle for me. It was time to let go.

In Matthew 11:28–30, we find that our journey with Christ provides rest and ease. He takes the burdens we were never meant to carry! In a world where we must be constantly "on," and people view us through a screen that doesn't show the reality of what we are going through or who we truly are, we can find rest and peace in Jesus. We don't have to have it all together, and I am here to tell you that no one does. I had to be reminded in my sorrow that He gives rest. He is gentle and humble in heart. And the burden is light when we

> *I just needed to trust Him and be obedient to His asks, and He would fight the battle for me. It was time to let go.*

surrender our life to Him (Matthew 11:30). The devil wants us to live in fear because it quiets our voice and keeps us in the midst of chaos, preventing us from living in freedom from shame and guilt.

Just like the woman at the well, the woman I was before I met Jesus, I am reminded that the thirst we have is only satisfied by what He offers—living water. During a time of adversity, I found myself trying to satisfy my needs with what the world offered. I

> *There is hope that no matter what struggle or sin you are dealing with, it doesn't define you or have to be the final chapter in your story.*

love the picture Psalm 42:1 (NLT) paints, especially when I feel lost. "As the deer longs for streams of water, so I long for you, O God." This verse has become a reminder to seek Him. The power of grace can literally rewrite our stories, and when we call out to God, He never leaves us; we just need to seek Him. The Bible arms us with weapons to fight when we face trials. I would encourage you to spend time in Ephesians Chapter 6 to hear God's truth and restate your claim! There is hope that no matter what struggle or sin you are dealing with, it doesn't define you or be the final chapter in your story.

SURRENDER THAT LEADS TO TRUE OBEDIENCE

Tamra Andress, a good friend and fellow author, shares that we are "always becoming." My journey of sanctification has been one of constant surrender. There have been highs and lows, victories and defeats, but God has gone before me, and He will continue to fight for me. It's been over twenty years since my "at the cross" moment and only a few years since I found myself in a season of despair. Jesus has shown me the qualities I need to live a life of abundance: forgiveness, compassion, patience, humility, love, and obedience, just to name a few. For most of my walk with Him, I have leaned into the trait of compassion to guide my steps. Being compassionate has led me to forgiveness, gentleness, and love. When you've been hurt and can have compassion for those who have hurt you, true healing can happen.

With that said, in my new season of sanctification, I have found myself embracing the strength Jesus shows through His obedience because when left to myself, I will tear down all the beautiful things God has blessed me with. As my relationship with Him continues to grow, He has uncovered an area that needs refinement. As shared in the book I referenced previously, *More Than Enough: The Silent Struggle of a Woman's Identity*, my Type A personality tries to control outcomes. It's not easy for me to surrender full control without trying to take it back when faced with trials. It's through this weakness of mine that I feel strong, knowing He's in control. I have found through obedience that I can live fully surrendered to His will for my life. The freedom I have found is like no other, and it is there for you too!

Christ is obedient.

"When you obey my commandments, you remain in my love, just as I obey my Father's commandments and remain in his love" (John 15:10, NLT).

"Even though Jesus was God's Son, he learned obedience from the things he suffered" (Hebrews 5:8, NLT).

Where do you need to be obedient to His will for your life, and what are you holding onto that needs to be surrendered to God or to someone you love that could lead to your freedom in Christ Jesus?

pray

Reflect

VICTORIA CIRESI is an HR business consultant and co-author of two best-selling books, *More Than Enough: The Silent Struggle of a Woman's Identity* and *The Joy-full Entrepreneur: Awaken, Renew, Transform: Combatting Business Myths, Armoring Up with Truth*. Her career journey has been shaped by a deep passion for helping small businesses build thriving cultures by guiding their people strategy. With experience as a business owner and former executive leader for a large boutique fitness franchise, she brings practical insights and support to leaders seeking growth and navigating change.

Victoria focuses on simplifying complex challenges and offering actionable guidance that drives meaningful, lasting results. She views her work as an opportunity to serve others by empowering them to unlock their potential and create positive impact in their lives and workplaces.

Faith, family, and ministry are central to Victoria's life. She strives to keep God at the center of everything she does, prioritizing her roles as a wife, mother, and leader of Casa Gioiosa (Joyful Home), a ministry devoted to prayer, serving meals to those in need, and guiding women through devotionals. Victoria resides in Charlotte, North Carolina, with her husband and three sons and is committed to living with purpose, staying rooted in gratitude, and finding joy in every part of her journey.

The transformation from our sinful human nature into a sanctified (holy) being is a beautiful thing, but it is often a messy process. Like a cocoon releasing a butterfly, we evolve from our old nature into something spectacular. This process is only achieved with the help of God himself but requires our cooperation.

Jenny Ingels

Chapter 2

My Undivided Heart

By Jenny Ingels

The transformation from our sinful human nature into a *sanctified* (holy) being is a beautiful thing, but it is often a messy process. Like a cocoon releasing a butterfly, we evolve from our old nature into something spectacular. This process is only achieved with the help of God himself but requires our cooperation.

In Ephesians 4:22–24 (NIV), we are taught to put off our old self and put on the new self. "You were taught, with regard to your former way of life, to put off your old self, which is being corrupted by its deceitful desires; to be made new in the attitude of your minds; and to put on the new self, created to be like God in true righteousness and holiness."

What does it really mean to leave our old ways behind? Clearly, it cannot be what the world offers us, that which corruption and sinfulness promise and profess are good. For these things are incompatible with what is righteous and holy. Our limited view of God's immense power is a shadow of the gift of life everlasting. This eternal covenant of restoration, promised in the Garden, supersedes all human understanding and takes us behind the veil, where we are at the Father's feet. It's a supernatural place where we can listen to His voice as He tells us the truth.

The world asks us to hold on to what it offers by seeking wealth, success, and prosperity, but these things are just masquerading as truth. Christ calls us to store up our treasures in heaven (Matthew 6:20), hidden from the eyes of man but clearly visible to God. If I am to please man, I am not serving my Father. I serve Him alone, which is often a lonely walk from an earthly perspective. But there is nothing lonely about being with our Creator. He reveals the hidden treasures and makes our way straight (Isaiah 45:2–3). Faith takes us on an adventure unlike any other as we learn to let go and allow the author of life to write (right) our story.

Scripture tells us, "Above all else, guard your heart, for everything you do flows from it" (Proverbs 4:23, NIV). Yet, God is love, and Jesus commanded us to love Him above all else and love others as ourselves (Mark 12:30–31), including our enemies (Matthew 5:44). In action, this giving of love—our hearts—to people (including those who are against us) can leave us wounded. Personally, I have given my heart to many things, including people and pursuits that didn't earn it or deserve it. Some of these people used and abused it. Many ideals disappointed my heart, and some dreams I let my heart long for, in the end, weren't worth it. When the affairs of life shatter and scatter our hopes, faith gets shaken. It leaves us questioning what our priorities are and why they matter to us at all. I heard someone say a long time ago that we only get truly disappointed in life when we expect more of others than they do of themselves. Like many, I have issues with trusting people. I've been lied to and stolen from, cheated, deceived, and mistreated. I measure intent by actions, not words. I believe a person more by what they do than by anything they have to say.

As a child, I had a friendship heart necklace I shared with a best friend. We both wore half of it, and when we were together and combined those two halves, they made a whole heart. This seemed clever to a young girl, but life breaks and divides our hearts into many more pieces than the two halves of a metal charm. Broken and bruised hearts are much more painful, messy, and complicated than a single, simple cut or curvature of lines. It took me four decades to figure out a heart can only be made truly whole by the One who designed it. Only God knows what is needed for our hearts to be healed, protected, and restored to a strength that is unshakable and a faith that is unbreakable.

All four of my sons stole my heart before they were born. I could feel the pulse of blood flowing between them and me when they first fluttered inside my womb. Family, friends, acquaintances, and even strangers have warmed my heart and filled it with joy and contentment over the years. They have also hurt it, leaving it battered and tattered from their words, actions, or deeds that seemed to stab too deep. Death, disease, and injuries brought my heart to its knees more times than I can count, leaving me reeling, confused, and misaligned. I've questioned life and God's purposes. I've doubted my choices, desires, goals, and aspirations and second-guessed myself, my instincts, and my personal morals.

A well-intentioned girl grew into a woman who found it easy to fall in love and even easier to fall apart. I know I'm not unique in my perspective. Some people have stronger constitutions and more resilient spirits. I assume they can look upon the misuse and abuse of their hearts by others and count them as useful or useless without misgivings. But for me, I need more time to reflect. I desire a deeper understanding. I want to truly grasp why someone would take my love, affection, kindness, gentleness, trust, and generosity—my heart—and stomp all over it.

I recognize I may be guilty of the same—walking away from people I can no longer look in the eye. The pain, regret, and disappointments sometimes run deeper than my forgiveness, so I pray instead for God to fill the gap, bridge the divide, and heal the brokenness. Some scars have left marks I'd rather not recall. They require supernatural abilities beyond my capacity to heal. I put them on God's altar rather than leaving them to my own understanding or comprehension.

Over the past month, the heart has been the topic of several conversations I've had. It seems many people around me are battling physical ailments of the heart. A child in my son's school needs a heart transplant. I was told the problem was something she was born with, but it has worsened. I asked God, "What broke her heart?" As I still wait for an answer and pray for His miracle to heal her, my aunt is battling her frailty. She recently went to the hospital for a heart problem that left her with a pacemaker. Days later, she experienced ministrokes and uncontrollable blood pressure issues.

I was reminded that life and the heartbeats gifted to us, which only God can accurately count, are beyond our control. God holds the cards, numbers our years, knows the hairs on our heads, and ultimately wants our hearts, not just the physical part but the souls attached to them. The heartbeat, in conjunction with the breath in our lungs, defines life. Our pulse is an indicator of life itself. We declare someone deceased when their heart fails to beat, their pulse is gone, and signs of life depart. Yet, we tap dance around conception to suit some narrative for ourselves about when life truly begins. While man plays a part, it's in God's divinity that life begins and ultimately ends. Therefore, a miraculous God gives us a heart to beat and a soul to desire His presence in our lives. But the fall of creation in Eden allowed a great deceiver to lay a path of destruction, one shrouded in lies that keep us distracted still today.

We look to other people, demonic influences, passionate pursuits of the world, and our personal desires for accolades, titles, and success to define who we are. When this begins and continues, we seek purpose, meaning, and contentment in lesser things rather than in God. When it's not all bad, we call it good. When it appears all good, we often call it great. And when it falls apart, we blame fate. But maybe, just maybe, God designed it this way so we could taste and see His goodness, desire His closeness, seek His will, and search for Him in our confusion, disorder, loneliness, fear, and hiding places.

After a recent prolonged season of crushing, I came to the end of myself, exhausted by all the world had enticed me with. These man-made offerings no longer held my attention. I'd had enough of the self-adoration and pleasure-seeking. I was tired of self-reflection and introspection. I wanted more of God and less of me. I wanted to know who He had really made me to be. What purpose did those hard lessons serve? Why had many of those dreams, relationships, and ambitions I'd sought after for so long fallen apart? It was clear that none of it was wasted, but it also held

> *What He really wanted from me and what only I could give Him was my heart.*

no real significance compared to God's hand in it. God was present in all the failures and foibles. What He really wanted from me and what only I could give Him was my heart.

I promised all four of my sons that for their sixteenth birthdays, I'd take them anywhere in the world they wanted to go. Life derailed those plans for my firstborn, so the summer before his senior year of high school, he and I took a trip to Colorado instead. We hiked, white-water rafted, toured an aviation exposition, hung out with his best friend, and spent two nights enjoying concerts under the stars at a well-known amphitheater built on rocks.

A storm was rolling in when one of the main acts took the stage for the second night. This musician had recently undergone heart surgery, and he recalled a conversation with God where he was asked, "Do you trust me with your heart?" His trust in that situation was focused on the physical surgery, but God challenged him to consider the spiritual heart—the one where loyalty to the King is undivided. As he shared this experience and posed that same question to the audience, the sky broke open with an outpouring of rain, thunder, and lightning. It was as if God had asked the question himself and added an exclamation point.

The concert was immediately canceled, and the venue was evacuated. My oldest, bravest son and I made our way back to the car through this torrential downpour, being extra careful not to slip in our descent while I covered my head and prayed for safety with each unsteady step. My spirit nudged me. "That question was for you; do you trust me with your heart?" Flippantly, I thought, *Of course, I trust God with my heart*. But did I really?

Several months passed when I found myself on the road again. While launching the podcast *Pour It Out For Good*, I spent an evening in prayer and petition where my soul was reminded of the unanswered question from God, "Do you trust me with your heart?" This time, I was able to answer clearly, "No. I do not." Life had broken my heart more times than I could count, and my plans had frequently left me with bittersweet memories and photographs of times past. There was a grand design in all of it but also some major cracks, crevices, and divides I couldn't reconcile. The truth was, I didn't trust God with my heart at all. And, ouch—that hurt to admit.

I was guarding my heart, even from God, protecting it like He was out to break it. The following months brought me to a place where I could see so much of my past in technicolor dreams. It was clear I had a lot of dross around my heart. *Dross* is defined as waste, foreign matter, or impurities. In my case, it consisted of pain, intolerance, disappointments, discouragements, letdowns, and all the ugliness of life that had left their gunk behind. My heart was covered in "yuck," and it needed to be purified. When we fail to protect our hearts, this is the result. My heart had become something I no longer recognized. The Scriptures tell us in Proverbs 4:23 (NIV) to "Guard your heart, for everything you do flows from it." I had not done a good job of guarding my heart from life's encroachments.

> *I was guarding my heart, even from God, protecting it like He was out to break it.*

It's been nearly a year since that confession of not truly trusting God with my heart, but during that time, I realized all He ever wanted was the best for me. Revisiting that question once again, I can now say I trust Him with all my heart—not just part of it. It is not guarded *from* Him but shielded *by* Him. He has it all. I'm completely loyal and committed. The world's pursuits now seem meaningless to me. If my heart gets broken now, it's because I've asked Him to break my heart for what breaks His.

God's heart is broken by the affairs of this world and the people who ignore Him. I find my heart being broken frequently because of the pain all around me, and I want nothing less than His will, even when it seems terrifying. So I go where He sends me and follow when He calls. I want to step on the waters and not remove my gaze from Him, lest I start to sink. I want to believe in all His goodness, glory, and promises, not just some. With unwavering confidence and devotion, I want Him to reassure me continuously that He is always there, He has never left, and He will always be there—that no matter the cost or how tumultuous life's seas and storms may be, He's in it with me.

I want to say with the same fervor I once used against Him that I'm for Him. He has my full and total allegiance with a purified heart, free from dross and without wax—it's all His. He made my heart. He knows it intimately, and He knows what is best for me. And because I'm His daughter, whom He loves deeply, He won't mistreat it, deceive it, or leave it, and He won't abandon me. *Jesus is trustworthy.* He is worth more than I could ever give. I don't have much to offer the King of everything, but now He has the one thing He really wanted from me: my undivided heart. And that undivided heart holds a love like His.

> "Guard your heart because everything you do flows from it"
> (Proverbs 4:23).

> "Love is patient, love is kind. It does not envy, it does not boast, it is not proud. It does not dishonor others, it is not self-seeking, it is not easily angered, it keeps no record of wrongs. Love does not delight in evil but rejoices with the truth. It always protects, always trusts, always hopes, always perseveres. Love never fails" (1 Corinthians 13:4–8, NIV).

Do you trust God with your heart?
Why or why not?

pray

Reflect

Write

JENNY INGELS is a podcaster, author, and speaker. Her work is fueled by her love for God, her husband, and her four sons, along with her family, friends, neighbors, and even strangers—a love that strives to emulate the love of Christ. Her previous career in law enforcement and years spent as the wife of a retired combat veteran often exposed her to the darkest sides of life. She and her husband dealt with the loss of many of his brothers-in-arms who took their lives and the death of her best friend, who drank herself into a coma. Years have passed, but the war has never really ended for her family as they continue to fight for the lives and livelihoods of service members and their families back home.

After her friend's death, Jenny reconsidered her decades-long relationship with alcohol, but it took ten more years and a breast cancer diagnosis before she finally threw away her drinking "blanket." God's grace brought her to and through this life-altering transformation. Tired of going to untimely funerals and recognizing that alcohol was "the" catalyst for so many sins, she found she could alter her life for the greater good by putting it back in its proper perspective. As a result, she left her career to start the mission and write her testimony: Pour It Out For Good.

Understanding how the power of sharing our testimonies has an eternal impact and a biblical calling in the book of Revelation, she started the podcast *Pour It Out For Good* (www.pouritoutforgood.com). The mission has grown beyond a microphone into a mobilized campaign, inviting people into a thought-provoking analysis of how our cultural norms, societal pressures, and biblical misconceptions have shaped our use and abuse of all things destructive. Targeted to those who know how to fail but have a heart to win, her organization (www.pouritoutforgood.org) confronts the issues negatively impacting our lives and the lives of those we love. By switching the narrative, remembering the past, and hearing the truth, we alter our mindsets and change the course of history. When our better influence meets action, there is real impact.

Sanctification is the process of God guiding us to maturity by renewing our minds, hearts, and desires for the purpose of displaying Christ to the world.

Jennifer Beeman

Chapter 3

When Forgiveness Feels Offensive

By Jennifer Beeman

Sanctification is the process of God guiding us to maturity by renewing our minds, hearts, and desires for the purpose of displaying Christ to the world.

JESUS ENCOUNTER: HIS ANSWER WAS YES

Moving day was finally here! After over a month's wait, our little family would have a nice place in a safe neighborhood with a community garden, and the dream of living in the country, just minutes from the beach, would be fulfilled. We pulled up in the driveway to find our home occupied by another family. Anger, fear, and dread washed over me. My body started to shake as my blood pressure rose. For a brief moment, I sensed God trying to whisper to me, but I was too fired up to listen. We had planned out our expenses to the dollar. We had one last check coming from my previous employer and had paid our first month's rent, a deposit, and half of the following month's rent at the request of our landlord. We had no other options but to move in! Multiple attempts were made to contact the landlord, with no response.

My thoughts and emotions quickly unraveled as my pulse pounded in my throat and my stomach turned in knots. We decided to search the property for other management, landlords, or anyone who could explain what was happening. We found a group of maintenance workers who asked if "they" had stolen our money too. I questioned the man, "You know about this? Have they done this before? How do they get away with this, and why isn't the law involved?" One of the workers finally reached the landlord by phone and was instructed to tell us to leave the property or the authorities would be called; we were trespassing. Trespassing? We paid for the right to live here and had a signed contract to prove it! It was between panicky breaths and threats of nearly all kinds flying out of my mouth when God leaned in and whispered, "Forgive them."

"You can't be serious!" I blurted out loud, with an eye roll toward the sky.

God leaned in again and whispered, "I have a bigger purpose, but you need to forgive them now."

I knew this was God for three reasons: the message was firm and kind, based on biblical principles, and the opposite of my current emotions—the calm in the storm. My breath slowed, but the fire inside still burned with the pain of our current reality. "So, what you're telling me, God, is that they left us broke and homeless in a new town with a baby and a cat in the dead of winter, and you want me to tell them I forgive them? Just like that?"

His firm and loving answer was "Yes."

EVER THE GENTLEMAN: AN UNFORGIVING SERVANT

Jesus was inviting me to sink deeper into His kindness, reflecting a posture that was more accurately aligned with His character. His request for me to extend forgiveness was an invitation for all involved to see firsthand how He can make all things work together for the good of those who love Him and are called according to His purpose

> *Jesus was inviting me to sink deeper into His kindness, reflecting a posture that was more accurately aligned with His character.*

(Romans 8:28). Forgiveness is the perfect example of what it means to follow Jesus. He came that we might be restored and renewed. We are forgiven for everything because of what He did on the cross. That forgiveness is greater than anything we could accomplish on our own. It was the next step in my journey of sanctification. I was learning to love like Christ and "re-present" Him to the world as His representative. The process was messy and far from over.

Ever the gentleman, Jesus kept whispering, "Forgive them."

And my constant response: "I hear you, but why would you let them off for this? We are not their only victims; they need to be stopped."

This conversation continued for a few weeks while we bounced from hotel to motel to keep our family safe. The threat of theft was constant in the locations we could afford, and everything we owned was in our truck. We were allowed some assistance with food, and our tax return had just come in. Those resources provided us with enough to live on until Hubby-to-be could find a job. Each time Jesus whispered to forgive them, I felt a softening in my heart toward the landlord. I felt like one of those large shredded wheat bars sitting in a bowl of milk. I was soaking in the nourishing milk of the Word and softening at the center. Unfortunately, my outer crust was still crunchy and unyielding. My intentional alone time with the Lord was growing more consistent. The shame and brokenness of my past had made me fickle with trusting others. This situation only served to support that behavior. Trusting Jesus to bring a solution that would be to my satisfaction did not include letting this matter slide by. I can handle this, Jesus; you just keep us safe.

Over the next few weeks, I exchanged several heated texts with the landlords, including threats about who would be sorrier at the end of this battle. One Sunday, I decided to approach them on their turf to get this straightened out. We showed up at their church—no safer place than surrounded and supported by fellow Christians who would be appalled at the reality of their fellow Christ-followers' actions. As it turned out, they were not there that week. Everyone we talked to was delighted we had met them and spoke only positively about them. They were dearly loved, and we were dearly dismayed. We never found the courage to say a bad word to anyone. But I had reached the limits of what I could take and planned to get our money back, no matter what. The divide between my closeness with God's voice and my desires grew larger. The legalistic thinking I had hidden behind for most of my adult life was no more evident than at this very moment. We decided to sue them.

I was certain they would not show up, and we would win this case based on their lack of attendance. After all, would you want to show up and face a judge with these charges? I felt a twinge of nausea and unease in my spirit as I filed the paperwork and again as I paid the $120 fee. We only had about $300 to our name, which had to last for an unknown amount of time, so the financial gamble was big but nearly a sure bet. That twinge of unease returned with each action I took in preparation for the court date. Along the way, I started talking to God again. More importantly, I started listening again. I was sure He was asking me to stop the process, but I was unyielding to His request.

Jesus warns us about such unforgiveness in the parable of the unforgiving servant. In Matthew 18:23–27 (NIV), Jesus tells us, "Therefore, the kingdom of heaven is like a king who wanted to settle accounts with his servants [God and us]. As he began the settlement, a man who owed him ten thousand bags of gold was brought to him. . . . At this the servant fell on his knees before him. 'Be patient with me,' he begged, 'and I will pay back everything.' The servant's master took pity on him, canceled the debt and let him go [What Jesus does for us]." The rest of the parable depicts the same man, who had just been forgiven the impossible debt, immediately demanding repayment from others for meager debts owed to him. I was being that unforgiving servant (ouch!).

BECOMING LIKE CHRIST: A JACOB MOMENT

As the day approached, I felt sick to my stomach. I was not accustomed to standing up for myself, and doing it in court was wreaking havoc on my nerves. I still had the chance to leave and not see this through. I was no longer hearing His whispers, but I was sensing His disagreement in my spirit. I chose to show up and entered the courtroom with my file in hand and a sigh of relief. They were not there. We won by default. The judge reviewed my case file and determined we were owed $735. I walked out of the courtroom, feeling as though I was the guilty one. Dear God, what had I done? Despite the heaviness of guilt, I met with the clerk and asked how to collect what we were owed. It never occurred to me that winning was no guarantee we would get paid. It was up to the defendant to make payment directly to the court, and they would send the money to us—$120 and time lost. But even more than that, I felt an intense sense of shame surround me.

This moment was a reminder of Jacob, the son of Isaac. He struggled in his dealings with God and man. Jacob's propensity to manipulate situations for his benefit often contrasted with God's character. Jacob refused to give up, and God wrenched Jacob's hip out of the socket to end the struggle (Genesis 32:25). I had come to that pain point, and, like Jacob, I would have to limp home. I spent a few days in guilt and tears before the Lord, telling Him how sorry I was for hurting His daughter. The process of sanctification, leading me toward the right decisions, guiding me to repentance, and ultimately testifying to His divinity, was well underway! God was fully committed to our sanctification before we were fully submitted to Him.

God was fully committed to our sanctification before we were fully submitted to Him.

A hope that I could undo the court's decision compelled me to call the court and request the ruling be dropped. I pleaded with the clerk and explained how we forgave them the debt, and it was no longer owed. I was told, at that point, what's done is done; it could not be changed. I had finally reached the end of myself, my selfishness, and my stubborn will. I decided to do what God had been asking of me all along. I had to tell her we had forgiven the debt. I was fearful of the reaction I might receive if I were to call, so I opted to text her the good news of forgiveness. I clearly stated this forgiveness was a direct result of God's request. Her response was overwhelmingly kind and full of thanksgiving. In full disclosure, I explained how my call to the court had confirmed that the ruling remained and shared that we would not pursue her for payment. Each step of obedience brought a new measure of peace and a release from the weight of the shame that encompassed me.

Almost immediately, we saw the release of blessings in our lives. It wasn't long before Hubby-to-be was offered a job with a well-known delivery company, providing us stability and a significant increase in income. The next step was to find suitable housing. The mobile home we lived in lacked basic heat and air, and we had a colony of ants living inside and outside our walls. We battled the ants and hand-washed all our clothing, including cloth diapers. We were flat broke and eager to move on from the mess that was finally behind us.

We made an effort to view every available place for rent where we felt our credit history (which included much more debt than we had just forgiven) would be accepted. One afternoon, after looking at almost everything we could find, I felt the "holy nudge"—the instinct to do something that makes no sense but carries with it a sureness of success.

"Babe, turn in here," I whispered.

"Here? On the left? Those are really nice and close to the beach. I'm pretty sure we can't afford it," remarked Hubby-to-be.

"Just go," I urged softly. "There is something about this place. I don't know what, though." We pulled up to a fairly new apartment complex with a pool, walking trail, ponds, laundry facilities, and places to play with our daughter. We toured and shared a bit of our story. We loved the place. The leasing agent and manager offered to run our credit to see what would be required to move in. We did qualify but would need a double-down deposit and the first month's rent. We did not have that kind of money and figured the moment was over. We kindly thanked them for their time and wished them well. I was baffled. What had just happened? I was stunned and confused. I know I felt a holy nudge. What was the point of this exercise? As we slowly climbed into our truck, the manager came out, waving us down. She invited us back into the office, sharing that God told her to let us live there.

"Are you sure? We don't and won't have everything we need to move in," I shared, just in case she missed it the first time. The manager looked us in the eyes and stated confidently, "When God says to do something, you just do it. I will get it all worked out. Just give me what you have, and we will work something out for the rest." That sentence has been seared in my heart ever since. We were given the keys and a washer and dryer in our apartment. No more washing clothes and diapers by hand!

We quickly became good friends with the front office staff and began attending the same church. Hubby-to-be was baptized, and we soon found out our family was growing. Our stay was short-lived, as I was newly pregnant with our second child. We had complications with our first and knew this one would likely be the same. The breaking of the lease left a big bill behind, but our focus was on our daughters and heading home. We decided not to pay the bill, and by God's grace, we saw forgiveness for that debt and many others. The forgiveness, mercy, and grace we have experienced time and again far outweigh the small amount we forgave.

Christ is forgiveness.

Leaning into Jesus's profound forgiveness and compassion while on the cross assured me that even as I made my way through this situation, His love for me still existed. His *forgiveness* was for me too.

How would your life with Christ change if you chose to forgive that one thing you've been holding onto because of the "principle of the matter," and what might God reveal to you should you choose to let that person off the hook?

pray

Reflect

Write

JENNIFER BEEMAN resides in sunny Phoenix, Arizona, and holds the titles of wife, mother, and chaos coordinator. The traumas she experienced early in life left deep scars and led her to question her identity and purpose. She takes pleasure in recounting the distinctive ways in which God intervened and led her back to a connection with Him. She is currently pursuing her Bachelor of Arts in Communication and Interpersonal Relationships. She can often be found baking something yummy and playing barista in the church cafe.

Sanctification is the ongoing recognition of our desperate need for a Savior to rescue us from ourselves. It is the journey of transformation where God uses our struggles and brokenness to refine us, drawing us closer to Him. It is the process of learning to depend on God's grace in every moment, recognizing that our worth and identity are not rooted in our performance but in His unchanging love.

Kali Dunson

Chapter 4

Shame Is No Longer My Name
By Kali Dunson

Sanctification is the ongoing recognition of our desperate need for a Savior to rescue us from ourselves. It is the journey of transformation where God uses our struggles and brokenness to refine us, drawing us closer to Him. It is the process of learning to depend on God's grace in every moment, recognizing that our worth and identity are not rooted in our performance but in His unchanging love.

Utter ruin and devastating sadness enveloped me. Will I ever move past this? Will this ever stop hurting? Did I use up all the mercy I was allotted? Was this going to be my story? Was this what I'd be known for? I felt stuck, stuck in a situation I didn't ask for, stuck in a hurt I knew God could repair, stuck in longing for reconciliation, stuck in anger with myself for who I'd become, stuck in what couldn't be undone, and stuck in knowing the truth of His Word but not believing it. Would the brokenness ever mend?

I spent most of my life safeguarding myself from the possibility of anyone ever rejecting me. But despite my efforts, the inevitable happened, and there I was with tear-stained eyes, a weary heart, and nothing and no one to hide behind.

I was paralyzed in the wake of destruction, sitting in the wreckage of despair, and crying out to God, "When will you set me free? Is this the life I deserve? Will I ever move forward? Was I a mistake?" These were the painful questions that bled through my journal as I continued to question God. "What plan is this a part of? When will the weight of this pain stop being so heavy? God, do you see me? What if I trusted you this time, and you weren't enough? What if I am too broken? What if you don't come through for me?"

All my life, I learned that people would only accept me if I gave them the version of me they expected. Consequently, I believed this to be true about Jesus as well. Constantly seeking validation and approval, I was convinced that hiding my feelings of inadequacy was the only path toward acceptance, as if making my life look good on the outside would make me worthy on the inside. So I performed and masked my pain, terrified of people seeing my struggles. Yet, the more validation I sought, the emptier I felt. I longed to be told I was enough.

I was practically born in a church. We didn't have rules in our household; we had Scriptures "stapled" to our foreheads. Chores were paired with reciting, "This is the day the Lord has made; we will rejoice and be glad in it" (Psalm 118:24, NKJV) and "Do everything without complaining and arguing" (Philippians 2:14, NLT). Church attendance was expected, and participation was required. Of course, I "knew" Jesus. We talked every day. I'd pray to get an *A* on my tests. I'd thank Him for good health. I'd pray to feel peace about the decision I had already made and get His stamp of approval. God was only mad at me when I wasn't checking off my religious to-do list. Did I go to church this week? Nothing bad will happen. Did I lift my hands during worship? People knew I was dedicated. Did I read my Bible and memorize a verse? Oh, there must be a blessing somewhere in the week for me. My relationship was a transaction. I was in a state of restlessness—always trying to earn back the favor I thought I lost every time I messed up. As long as the good things I did outweighed the bad, I had earned my status as "a child of God."

So, to silence the inner voice that told me I was never good enough for God, I sought to mask it with the approval of others. I thought I'd feel worthy if I never let people down because if everyone accepted me, then nothing was wrong with me. Every encounter was a chance to prove my worth.

Acceptance was my drug. It broke me when someone didn't like me because that only validated the belief that something was deeply flawed within me. I believed that if I were good enough, then I'd be happy. I'd be loved. I'd be secure. I spent my whole life chasing things and people who would make me feel like I mattered.

Instead, I lost the safety net, the validation, I had always relied on for confidence and security. Going to church wasn't enough, reading my Bible wasn't enough, compliments from others weren't enough, money wasn't enough, my job wasn't enough, and my relationships weren't enough. Although my life looked full and even holy on the outside, I still felt utterly empty and alone when my head hit the pillow. Because I was more concerned with how *I* felt, I was ignoring the depravity of my heart. I was so busy filling my life with the approval of others that once their validation halted, it seemed as though I had hit rock bottom.

I felt like the woman in the Bible who bled for twelve years and faced profound isolation and shame (Luke 8:43–48). Her story resonates deeply with my own experiences of feeling unworthy and being an outcast in society. In Jewish culture, blood was unclean. So for her to be seen by others, she was forced to hide her condition. She piled on garments, carrying them as a weight of unworthiness. Desperate to be accepted, she hoped to conceal her vulnerability and be seen as worthy.

The insecurities that spilled out of me stemmed from never feeling good enough, and while the woman hid beneath her garments, I hid beneath my successes, my religion, my personality, and the approval of others. I could become whoever I needed to be for acceptance. I thought covering my brokenness and relying on others to give me a sense of self-worth would make me "clean." I thought covering the emptiness I felt would prevent people from leaving me, disliking me, or

> *I thought covering the emptiness I felt would prevent people from leaving me, disliking me, or talking badly about me—but other people were never meant to love me into a sense of self-worth.*

talking badly about me—but other people were never meant to love me into a sense of self-worth. Just as the woman "had spent all her living on physicians, [and learned] she could not be healed by anyone" (Luke 8:43, ESV), I realized I could never be truly fulfilled by the approval of others, no matter how hard I tried.

In the fifth chapter of Mark, we read of the encounter between Jesus and this woman and the moment she reaches out in desperation—and faith.

> "And Jesus, perceiving in himself that power had gone out from him, immediately turned about in the crowd and said, 'Who touched my garments?' And his disciples said to him, 'You see the crowd pressing around you, and yet you say, "Who touched me?"' And he looked around to see who had done it. But the woman, knowing what had happened to her, came in fear and trembling and fell down before him and told him the whole truth" (Mark 5:30–33, ESV).

In that moment, surrounded by the crowd, Jesus's awareness of the woman's need illustrates a profound truth: He sees us in our brokenness. Jesus knew who touched Him. Before she decided to enter the city that day, He knew she would touch Him. Jesus saw her when she was struck with that disease. He saw her in the moments she cried out, wondering what she had done wrong to deserve this. He saw her when her dreams of living a "normal" life weren't fulfilled because of the shame she felt. He saw her when she was told she was an outcast from her family and society. He *knew* who touched Him.

Can you picture it? There were hundreds, if not thousands, of people pushing against Him. Have you ever been to Disney World during the late-night fireworks show? I imagine it was like that. You're breathing in someone else's oxygen. You can smell what they had for dinner that night. Jesus was walking through that kind of crowd. Yet, He stops because "someone" touched Him. Of course, someone touched Him. This woman could've easily shrunk back into the crowd and said, "No, another day. I'll get Him when He's alone." Yet, her shame was overtaken by utter desperation; she longed not only to be seen but to be healed. Mark 5:33 (ESV) says, "[She] came in fear and trembling." I imagine that she risked not only being seen by Jesus but also by everyone else for who she truly was—all that she had tried to hide.

In her desperation, she reached out for just a thread of Jesus, a sliver of hope, and He stopped everything because He saw *all* of her. He doesn't wait to know us and heal us once we've earned it. He sees us in the middle of it, knowing all that we're trying to keep inside and hide. He does the same with you and me. He knew about the sins we'd commit and try to hide as well as the ones we haven't even thought of committing yet. He is not surprised by our sins and chooses to love us still. What she feared most about being seen was rejection—her entire life story was marked by it. Yet, the desperation in her rejection was the catalyst for her healing. She believed she had to steal a moment with Jesus because she hadn't done anything worthy of His attention. Just as the woman discovered healing through her vulnerability, I began to realize that true acceptance comes from being fully known. Tired of hiding behind her garments and concealing her pain, she was willing to risk being seen by others so that Jesus would heal her. By confronting her fears of exposure, she uncovered the truth about her identity. Ultimately, what she was most afraid of—being seen for all she was—was the very thing she had to face to be healed. To uncover the truth about *Whose* she was, she had to be honest about *what* she was.

Have you ever felt that way—like you need to earn God's approval to catch His attention? I often believe God only works in me when I've earned it, but what about those moments when He's pressing deeper truths out of me? Even on my worst days, He is working. I'm not made right with Him because I do a good deed. Instead, the Spirit, through His kindness, chooses to produce goodness in me.

Just as God called the Israelites out of Egypt and into the wilderness, I, too, was in my own wilderness. Though freed from slavery and tyrannical oppression in a land of idols that distracted them from fully devoting their hearts to God, they began to grumble in this unfamiliar place. In the wilderness, they lost their comfort and security, mirroring my struggles. We often resist the very situations meant to draw us closer to God, but it's when we are forced out of our comfort that we transform. Sometimes, Jesus places us in uncomfortable circumstances to help us recognize our deep need for Him. Similarly, my wilderness experience became a revelation of my dependence on God, stripping away the comforts I had relied on.

What should have been a brief journey turned into a long, arduous trek. This wasn't about God toying with their emotions; it was about revealing His character, undistracted by the comforts they had relied upon. They found Him in the wilderness. He appeared to them and reminded them of His everlasting love and promise of redemption. Often, it's easier to remain in our metaphorical Egypt, complaining to God about what we lack, rather than venturing into the unfamiliar where we confront our need for Him, are forced to rely on Him, and face our shame. We would rather deny the fullness of His restoration and redemption in the wilderness, preferring the familiarity of a life filled with idolatry and false security. In our longing to return to our "Egypt," we are unwilling to admit our humanity and need for a God who rescues us not just from our circumstances but from ourselves.

I had suppressed the pain for so long because it was easier than facing the truth I believed about myself. I wanted to make the pain go away. I began to bargain: "But God, if I can just get their acceptance, if I can just get them to believe me or listen to me, then maybe they'll see I'm worthy—worthy enough to root for, stick around for, and fight for." Through malicious slander, isolation, and brokenness, there was purification, refinement, and healing. God had asked me to be still when all I wanted to do was stand up and defend myself. He asked me not to fight but to remain silent, not to correct them or change their minds about me but to trust that He was fighting my battles (Exodus 14:14)—to trust that everything that comes against me has to work *for* me (Romans 8:28). It wasn't until God whispered, "Their acceptance will never be enough," that I found peace in the wilderness.

He led me to a place where my only hope was Him. All I wanted was provision—a way out—because then I could trust Him in the storm. But what if there wasn't a way out? What if I were to deal with the outcast, the hurt, and the insecurities for the rest of my life? Would I still trust Him? Could I still believe He is good?

I wasn't confident in who I was or what I wanted. I was more dependent on the system than the "Source." Because I was filling my life with so much noise, I missed the stillness, and in the stillness, I didn't recognize the closeness of our Father's presence. I was so busy muting the pain of imperfection that I missed the song of grace He'd been singing over me. Life had seduced me. Words had enticed me. But Jesus was whispering to me. In my despair, I heard His voice calling me back to His arms.

He called me out into the wilderness so He could whisper to me. He called me out of my routines. He called me out of the comfort of control until everything was drained from me, and I could only find satisfaction in knowing Him. This whisper in the wilderness reminded me that true provision comes not from trying to escape the pain but from knowing who He is—delighting in Him and being fulfilled and satisfied by Him. God used my deepest hurts to rename me and draw me back into a relationship with Him. Just like the Israelites when they left Egypt, I didn't know how each day would unfold; I only knew I had to wake up and seek Him earnestly, trusting that my safety, sustenance, satisfaction, and every need depended on Him.

> *God used my deepest hurts to rename me and draw me back into a relationship with Him.*

God is active in the exile. He moves through our pain, bringing hope and healing, even when we feel undeserving. He can even bring you out of the brokenness you intentionally walked into. He is working on your behalf, even if you aren't on "good terms" with Him. You are not alone. Nothing can stand against the Lord. Redemption isn't just for those who earn it. The acceptance you've been searching for is in His presence.

Often, it was easier for me to carry on by hiding behind my flaws. However, I felt a call to surrender and trust Him completely. He called me to release the need for approval from others and to find stillness—a difficult but necessary step for my healing. He asked me to trust Him with my life and the opinions others held of me, urging me to release the need to control what they believed and said about me.

I wish I could say that hitting rock bottom transformed me completely, but instead, I felt more broken and ashamed than ever and less like myself than before. I had been filling my life with gifts instead of the Giver, and I wouldn't have run back to Jesus if He hadn't taken away the false comforts I clung to. Yet God always hedges on the side of mercy. This is proven in His call for repentance and redemption. He never once gave up on me. He is always drawing us near.

I'd love to say it worked out perfectly and that I don't care what other people think about me. I'd also love to tell you that everyone came back into my life, and we have lived happily ever after. But that's not what happened because God doesn't promise us those things when we follow Him. It's not a one-time decision where everything will turn out exactly as we imagined. Following Jesus is a journey, not a destination.

To this day, I still hurt over the relationships lost, the choices made, and the words spoken. I mourn over the life I lost. But you know what? I think that's okay. I think it's okay to hold two opposing feelings at once. I think it's okay to grieve over what was lost and be thankful for the redemption of what's to come. On this side of my brokenness, I know Jesus deeper, share grace quicker, and am willing to embrace honesty about who I am and my struggles. I didn't gain a whole new friend group that worshiped the ground I walked on or instantly woke up loving everything I saw in the mirror. I wasn't magically healed or left without a care in the world. Instead, this road has been one of the loneliest roads I've ever journeyed. But this I can say with all my heart: Jesus sees me, He is with me, and I am intimately known and accepted by Him, and that brings greater satisfaction than any person can provide.

Through God's mercy, I began relying on the stability and security of His presence rather than being dependent on the faulty and wavering approval of others. But for me to see how needy I was, I had to become desperate. Desperation, while uncomfortable, led me to the profound love and acceptance that only He can provide. Like a good shepherd, He had to break my legs to carry me home.

Christ is El Roi—the God who sees me. Amidst my brokenness, sorrow, and shame, Christ saw me. Like Sarai (who tried to take matters into her own hands in Genesis by commanding her servant to give her children), many of us try to fill in the gaps where we think God has forgotten us. We try to fill the voids within us through materialism, work, love, and approval so we don't have to face the parts of ourselves we don't like.

Many of us feel like Sarai (Genesis 16:1–3); we believe God forgot to come through on His promise. Others may feel like Hagar (Genesis 16:6–13), trapped in an impossible situation and surrounded by contempt and cruelty. Both of these women felt unseen because of their circumstances. Yet, even when they tried to hide their shame, the Lord met them in their darkest moment. He saw them. If I were to only tell you one thing today, dear reader, it would be this: my God is a God who sees you intimately and fully, without judgment or disappointment. He is a father whose arms are open, whether the circumstances you're in are caused by the cruelty of others, your own decisions, or the fact that we live in a fallen world. The Lord is *El Roi*—the God who sees you, loves you, and accepts you for all that you were, are, and will be.

> "He pays even greater attention to you, down to the last detail—even numbering the hairs on your head!" (Matthew 10:30, MSG).
>
> "You keep track of all my sorrows. You have collected all my tears in your bottle. You have recorded each one in your book" (Psalm 56:8, NLT).

Have you ever found yourself in a transactional relationship with God, feeling the need to earn His approval or the approval of others, especially during times of misunderstanding or shame, and, if so, how did that experience shape your understanding of vulnerability and acceptance?

pray

Reflect

Write

From an early age, Kali believed she had to earn the love of others by maintaining the image that was expected of her—perfection. Growing up as a pastor's kid, she learned to mask her failures with religious performances. Life quickly became a balancing act of staying true to herself while juggling the aching desire to be accepted by others. The pain of heartbreak and rejection led Kali to a place of brokenness that pushed her closer to God and to the realization that she needed to be rescued—she needed a Savior. By embracing her vulnerability and acknowledging her brokenness, she experienced freedom in Jesus. She learned that true acceptance doesn't have to be earned; instead, it comes from her heavenly Father, who draws near to us with compassion and mercy.

Kali brings a diverse background of experience to her work, blending her passions for outreach, community, and connection. As an outreach coordinator, she partners with local churches to help them connect with organizations in order to serve their communities. Her background as a teacher has equipped her with valuable communication skills, which she has leveraged as a marketing and brand manager for large companies and enterprises. In addition to her roles as a passionate blogger and published author of online articles, Kali runs her own business, where she serves as a marketing consultant, graphic designer, content creator, and brand manager, helping clients bring their visions to life.

Most importantly, Kali finds joy in hearing and telling the powerful stories of grace and restoration Jesus writes in her life and the lives of those around her. She is passionate about seeing the captives set free and being an advocate for the voiceless and outcasts. Her heart's deepest desire is to see the people of God rise up and genuinely love those around them. With a mind constantly filled with big dreams to change the world and a spirit that's always up for fun, she's a whirlwind of passion and excitement. Kali's life is full of adventure and chaos. She is a wife to her best friend and the most patient man she ever dreamed of marrying. Together, they have four beautiful kids. You can find her sipping coffee outside with her husband, chasing her kids around, burying her head in a good book, dancing in the kitchen, or laughing loudly. Kali's vibrant spirit and action-packed life inspire those around her to embrace life's adventures with joy and love.

Sanctification is the lifelong process of knowing God and being transformed by the knowing of God.

Becky Vasquez

Chapter 5

Sandcastles
By Rebekah (Becky) Vasquez

*S**anctification* is the lifelong process of *knowing* God and being transformed by the *knowing* of God.

I grew up by the beach and spent many days in the sun-kissed sand. It is one of my favorite places on Earth. Growing up, my family would set up chairs and umbrellas near the shore, and we would play from sun up to sun down! Some of us would brave the waves, while others would spend hours meticulously building castles or forts made of sand. As the day progressed, the tide would go out and come in, only to sweep away the precious sandcastles we tirelessly constructed under the canopy of the sun.

As children, we naively thought the sand would hold. We trusted our creations were safe from the crashing waves, the potential paws of a furry friend, and the occasional foot of a feisty sibling! Much like castles in the sand, we can put our trust and hope in the things we build with our hands, only to see them come crashing down. The circumstances we face and the seasons we endure often reveal the true nature of what or whom we place our trust in.

> *The circumstances we face and the seasons we endure often reveal the true nature of what or whom we place our trust in.*

As I sat to write and share my story, I realized the countless moments when Jesus met me in the middle of my fragile sandcastles. People ask me, "So when did you give your life to Jesus?" Honestly, I feel like I was birthed knowing about Him. He has always been present in my life. Some would say I "teethed" on Bible stories, worship services, and prayer meetings. I am a PK (i.e., a pastor's kid) through and through, and I will always be so grateful for my parents and those who helped disciple my walk with Jesus at such an early age.

There are finite moments, though, when the great faith of our parents grows cold, extinguished by the undeniable feelings of raw and real soul pain. These are the moments where we are blindsided by life and drink the cup of agony, pain, rejection, or disillusionment. These are the moments where we question everything we believe. We question the validity of our core beliefs, and our castles made of sand are revealed.

So, if you would, allow me to give you some context by sharing parts of my story—moments of my testimony—before I *truly knew* Jesus. These are just some of the sandcastles I built in the different seasons of my life, where I came face to face with the real, unfiltered, and relational Jesus.

It was the Fall of 2011, and my husband of six years came to me and said, "Babylove, I want to become a Navy SEAL." Now, to give you a little more context, when we met and began dating four years earlier, I told him I would *not* marry a man who was in the military (ahhh, never say never)! I couldn't imagine being away from someone I loved for months at a time, and *most* of our military friends were getting divorced, experiencing infidelity, falling into the traps of alcoholism and substance abuse, or dying. I had a fear-based bias of entering the military lifestyle! Anxiety and worry became my daily companion as I struggled with the idea of my reality changing so quickly.

One weekend, I attended a women's retreat where the use of electronic devices was not allowed, immersing us in a quiet space for reflection with God. I remember pacing the grounds, telling God how angry I was at Him for putting this desire in my husband. Didn't He know I couldn't do this? Didn't He know this would wreck our family? The more I worried, the more fear came in like a flood. My heart rate elevated, and I found myself on my knees in an empty room next to a row of old wooden church pews. I glanced up and saw that I was enveloped in sunlight pouring through a weathered, stained glass window, illuminating an old, rugged cross. Amid the empty void created by my fears, I dropped to my knees and cried out to God. As my tears soaked the carpet, I suddenly felt a warm presence enveloping my body—a familiar sensation reminiscent of the sun-kissed warmth I experienced as a child by the ocean shore. And in a calm, steady voice, God spoke. He reminded me of who He is and who I am to Him. He shared His plans for my family, and as He tended to every detail of my heart, my fear and worry began to evaporate. At that moment, I surrendered all of my plans, my husband, and my castles made of sand. I came home to my husband and told him what God had said, and tears welled up in his eyes. So, with God at the helm, we set our sails to the wind, and with surrendered hearts, we followed God's plan.

In 2012, my husband went off to basic training, BUD/s Prep, and BUD/s. He left a couple of days after our daughter's first birthday. Our oldest son had just turned five. That year, we saw him in person for maybe three weeks. During training, he suffered a serious injury when a three-hundred-pound log struck the side of his head. At 3:00 a.m., I received an unexpected call. With a tone of regret and pain, he said, "I rang out." Despite his injury, he wasn't allowed to roll back to the next class because of his age—he was thirty-one and had already come in on a waiver. Instead, he spent three more months in medical care in San Diego before being stationed back in our hometown. We finally had Daddy home . . . but five days later, they stationed him on an aircraft carrier, and he deployed for eleven months. I remember thinking, "How will I survive this? How will our marriage sustain the distance? How can the kids grow up confident without their father home?" (Another wave rolled in . . . revealing more sandcastles.)

As we entered another season apart, we faced new challenges—those invisible struggles that can't be easily resolved. The daily difficulties of parenting alone, the strain of a distant marriage, and the grief over my husband's lost sense of purpose weighed heavily on us. He was angry with God and far from home, trapped in the belly of a metal ship. He could only call home about once a month. During those conversations, I heard troubling stories of sailors cheating on their spouses and visiting overseas brothels—and even instances of suicide.

Once again, I found myself captive to fear, worry, and doubt. I struggled to grasp what was happening and questioned why God led us down this path if my husband's dream of becoming a SEAL wasn't meant to be realized. Was my family going to be just another divorce or suicide statistic? So I laced up my running shoes and went out for a run, filled with anger and disillusionment and blaming God for the wave of disappointment crashing over me. About thirty minutes into my run, the sky opened up, and it poured! It was the kind of downpour where you could barely see two feet in front of you. As I ran, drenched in sorrow and unbelief, I cried out to God. "Where are you?! How could you leave me alone in this?" As I ran faster, God met me in the middle of my pain and said, "Rebekah, RUN! Run, my love! Let the rain pour down! Let the pain come! RUN! Run into these arms! Though you're soaked to the bone, I will *never* leave you alone!" As I sprinted through the wind and rain, I felt my soul come alive as He softly spoke those words to me, filling me with the courage to press on.

It was the beginning of the Summer of 2022, and the past six months had been a blur of intense stress and emotional ups and downs. Our family had recently gone through a painful business partnership split that resulted in significant financial loss and strained one of our closest friendships. My husband and I didn't sleep for four months. But never in our wildest dreams could we have foreseen what this new season would bring upon us. . . .

It was a regular Saturday morning, but as I climbed out of bed, I fell straight to the floor. The room was spinning intensely, and I had no sense of which way was up or down. I tried to get up several times on my own but felt severely nauseous. I called out to my kids, and they found me on the floor, violently throwing up and crying out. Hours turned into days, days turned into weeks, but the debilitating effects of vertigo continued. Nothing took it away; nothing made it better. I sat in my room for hours, crying out to the Lord, and had to send my kids away to stay with family so my husband could care for me. I was so weak and dizzy that I couldn't manage even the most basic tasks, such as walking to the bathroom by myself. After some tests, I learned I had an inner ear infection, cervical vertigo, and a possible viral infection. It felt like the perfect storm, leaving me feeling helpless and disoriented.

There's something profoundly sobering about being unable to go to the bathroom on your own, pick up clothes off the floor, or even lift your head to read the Bible. Each small task that once felt trivial now seemed monumental. The simple, everyday tasks were an instant trigger that set off hours of nauseating spinning and made me very aware of how human and helpless I really was. After countless nights spent praying and pouring my heart out to God and getting postural therapy for the cervical vertigo, the sickness started to settle, and I began to find relief. And that is when the exhaustion set in. I realized my belief systems about God often depended on whether my family and I were okay. Even though He proved himself faithful over and over again, I had deep-rooted trust issues tied to self-reliance and the false belief that if I followed Christ, everything would—*should*—be good and work out for me. It was in those sobering days afterward, when I had no pride or plan left, that the *knowing* of Jesus was all that remained. He was everything to me as I lay bedridden and sick. He was my fortress and my safe place. He was my peace amid the raging storms, not my husband, not my job, not my family, not my ministry, not my reputation, and not even my health!

> *It was in those sobering days afterward, when I had no pride or plan left, that the knowing of Jesus was all that remained.*

You see, "before she *knew* Jesus" is not a one-time event. You can't find it within the walls of a church or even within the scholarly halls of a university or seminary. No, it's the journey of *knowing and being known by Jesus.* It's a relational journey we all are invited into. We can use religious or biblical terms, like *sanctification*, but the Hebrew translation is simple and freeing, and I would like to share it with you. God's Word says sanctification is the lifelong process of *knowing* God and being transformed by the *knowing* of God. (Read that again.) The Hebrew word *yada* (ידע), i.e., knowing, is not standing back and looking upon something from a distance or sitting in a classroom and regurgitating information. *Yada* (ידע) is an active, intentional, involved, experiential, and intimate word that is rooted in a relationship. It's knowing and being known, recognizing and perceiving, acknowledging and being seen, which can only be accomplished through intimately gained experiences.

I have to know (*yada*) God to be truly known (*yada*) myself. Our "being" is not informed by our doing, our knowledge, or our religious efforts to keep the law. Instead, knowing (*yada*) God informs our whole being. If we allow the knowing (*yada*) of God to inform our lives—the darkest parts of our stories, the painful circumstances we endure, the belief systems built on castles of sand, then we will experience a living God, our heavenly Father and Friend, the Shepherd and Lover of our souls, the God of our nights and our days, the Great Potter and Pruner of our being who will, by His hand, transform us from glory to glory! We will know Him, and He will know us. And in the knowing, we will experience an intimate, deeply rooted relationship that will outlast every crashing wave, sweeping tide, and self-made castle of sand. I could sit for hours telling you all the ways Jesus met me in my "befores" and how He has held and continues to hold my whole world together.

So, my friends, I leave you with my testimony of coming into a deeper understanding of *yada*, or "knowing" Him. *Christ is the firm foundation we can trust*, the rock upon which we can build our lives. Jesus is everything we need—completely worthy of our trust and affection in every season and passing tide.

I encourage you to invite Him into the intimate spaces and places of your heart, and as you journey forward, remember the power of God's word to guide and transform you. Hebrews 10:23 (AMP) reminds us: "Let us seize and hold tightly the confession of our hope without wavering, for He who promised is reliable and trustworthy and faithful [to His word]." And in Isaiah 41:10 (NIV), we find comfort: "So do not fear, for I am with you; do not be dismayed, for I am your God. I will strengthen you and help you; I will uphold you with my righteous right hand."

May these words encourage you as you walk the journey of faith, being transformed by the intimacy of knowing and being known by Jesus.

Think back to the times in your life, or maybe it's a season you are currently in, and ask yourself this question: What "sandcastles" have I built my life on because of fear or ego, how can I then turn toward and trust Jesus in this area of my life, and what castles made of sand do I need to lay down so that I can truly rely on Him?

pray

Reflect

Write

Rebekah, friends call her Becky, is a big-sky, sunset-on-a-beach, family-oriented, and Jesus-loving wife and mom! She enjoys all things creative that inspire the soul! From music to design, she has cultivated a love for the arts since childhood. With over twenty years of experience in the media, marketing, and design industry, she has created and helped launch countless designs, websites, and campaigns for entrepreneurs, corporate entities, nonprofits, and small businesses.

Her God-dream and passion is her family nonprofit called Build His House. It is dedicated to strengthening the family unit by helping families discover a path of restoration and hope in their relationships. Her long-term goal is to have land with a retreat center where families can come and reset to find hope and healing in their relationships. She is also the founder of the "Triggered Conference" and loves pouring back into the community through women and family-oriented ministry. She has a lifelong love for worshipping Jesus, diving into God's Word, and telling people about the transformative power of walking with Christ.

Sanctification, becoming like Jesus and being known by Jesus, isn't a one-off encounter or a good Sunday sermon. It's the leaning in when nothing makes sense in order to sense His existence in the void of senses.

Tamra Andress

Chapter 6

The Mess of the Making
By Tamra Andress

Sanctification, becoming like Jesus and being known by Jesus, isn't a one-off encounter or a good Sunday sermon. It's the leaning in when nothing makes sense in order to sense His existence in the void of senses.

As I sat overlooking the cascading rays that illuminated the picturesque mountain line of the continental divide from my hotel room in Denver (thousands of miles from home), another puzzle piece of God's beautiful mosaic was revealed to me. I thanked Him for the predestined space He had coordinated on my calendar. This was a *kairos* type of time that I had not prepared for or prayed into but was being gifted week by week amid an unexpected valley season. It felt like an expansion of space that I couldn't, even in my desperation, grasp hold of in my day-to-day, home-front calendar.

Kairos means "timeless" or "season" in Greek. The variation between chronos and kairos time is quantitative versus qualitative. Chronos time thrusts us into a time that will escape us, further ingraining within us a tendency to pack in every moment because of a multitude of fears: the fear of missing out, the fear of losing, and even the fear of success. Ultimately, this has us operating in a place of performance-based living while knowing and being known by God but not resting in Him. That's where kairos time offers expansion and eternal peace, even for a given moment. It's just not the systematic default of our society. Kairos time has an essence of eternal expansion, unlike the "it's too late" of chronos that can compound regret or hurriedness.

Busy is the worst four-letter word in the bunch because it carries so much baggage. I've avoided the concept, the hustle, the friction, and the tension since I met Jesus. . . . I pressed it away, even when the world preached it like a badge of honor. The moments when people mentioned, "I was moving too fast" or how "busy" I was would strike a nerve every time because of my people-pleasing, overdrive tendencies before I was made new in Christ. "You don't know me, and you don't know my God" would hum through my mind as I presented an alternative idea for them to grasp. Intentional: a choice to walk boldly into the time gifted rather than dragged along by a societal mechanism that keeps us distracted, defeated, and defiant. Time is a gift, and stewardship is our step of obedience to treasure that gift. Being busy represents a lack of discipline and self-control, which denotes disobedience. And though I have plenty of other areas to sharpen, I've felt confident in this space for quite some time, even when the occasional suggested "slow down" from a friend would leave a lingering sting in my intentional God-sized dream-building zone.

> *Intentional: a choice to walk boldly into the time gifted rather than dragged along by a societal mechanism that keeps us distracted, defeated, and defiant.*

That day in Denver, as the sunset mirrored back to me on my screen, I tried to capture its beauty in a picture. I couldn't help but take special notice of several steeples in my line of sight that had revealed themselves as if to say, "Less about the sunset and more about Me." He speaks in the most subtle and profound ways. I hadn't been this present in my rhythm in several weeks in terms of calendar, time, or even mental space. Perhaps it was the intimate release I had just experienced with my husband the night before. Perhaps it was the solitude without a pressing agenda of the day. Perhaps it was the sweet voices of my kiddos who had just captured the day in their evening prayers with me before signing off into their slumber. Perhaps it was the hours gifted back to me as I traveled into different time zones. Regardless, I caught my breath with gratitude. And it was the first time I felt fully alive in the valley that had become my life for the past several weeks. This was the ray of hope He had been wooing me to enter.

The Mess of the Making

Let me share the deeper meaning of this "ray of hope" visual that I'm holding tightly to in my mind's eye. At the beginning of this tragic period, God gifted me a vision I clung to every day. It was a vision of me in a valley, more youthful in appearance yet still at my present age. I had a radiance about me. I was standing in this piercing ray of sunshine that had penetrated the valley's treetop canopy, a canopy that ordinarily produced a dark and dreary landscape. But not this time. In this vision, God showed me the path ahead and what my journey would look like—tunnel vision. In an instant, I saw the entire valley and the truth that I would never be without Him. I saw pockets of sunshine but knew I'd *have* to walk through the dark spots. It was unavoidable and *intentional*. But I'd never be alone, and soon enough, I'd be back in the ray, lifting my chin and eyes to His radiance to refuel and give me enough momentum to make it through the next days of darkness. My stance was palms open, feet planted, and head to the sky, knowing He would be my recharge. It truly gave me a whole new meaning to the lyric "walking on sunshine."

I don't know about you, but walking with Jesus is one of the sweetest and most peculiar experiences. It's composed of fully anticipating that His tender thoughts will consume and protect you while also experiencing the moments of silence and the in-betweens where you spin in a childlike circle to catch His gaze—only to feel isolated, lost, or left behind once again. And though I walk with the secured confidence, based on historical proof, that He must not be too far away, this latter sense of isolation was where I found myself—amid a devastation I felt was closing in on me. Grief over circumstances shared by loved ones now threatened to snuff out the flicker of my flame while my soul thirsted for a reignite from Abba. "Where are you?" "Why now?" "Why couldn't we have done this sooner?" But a final question lingered: "Where am I responsible?"

Ownership: a unique piece to the *Always Becoming* journey. Once you've been walking with Jesus, past the stage of redemption and radical salvation moments, you start to recognize the relational nature of

> *Relationship requires recognition.*

our triune God. Relationship requires recognition. He is a teacher, savior, comforter, and friend (to name a few), all of which require a secondary interaction for effectiveness. A teacher needs a student. A savior needs a damsel. A comforter needs those to comfort. A friend needs a friend. Having this awareness of the two-to-tango dance with Jesus puts us not in a place to point fingers, accuse, call out, or demand but in a place to reflect, wonder, invite, and plead. Ownership is required for relationship. How could I have played a part in these unraveling situations? How did I end up in the valley, even though it doesn't feel like these predicaments are my fault?

He's never left or forsaken you. And in your surrender, He's always shaping you. Shaping, like the potter and His masterpiece, will often appear to be the "begin again" mess of a moment—starting from scratch, even with so much revealed understanding of preparation, process, plan, performance, partnership, and posture. Each restart isn't a failure. Instead, it is an opportune time to create the next work of art, putting into play the richer, deeper, molding-work wisdom of what surrender looks like beneath the Maker's hands.

Even as an entrepreneur with a high tolerance for risk, messy isn't my favorite adjective or step in the process. And yet, as a messenger, I'm well aware my *mess* is an intricate and vital part of the message. I'm okay with imperfect but messy . . . *sheesh*. Honestly, I had just personally resolved not to have this level of catastrophe to clean up again, especially after the monumental come-to-Jesus mess I had cultivated nearly a decade earlier (assisted by worldly pressures, secular influences, and the enemy's conniving support). My reasoning had been if I had a quarter-life crisis, I would avoid a midlife one.

But here I am in the mud, wrestling and anticipating, because I know my God is never unintentional or too busy to make me new. I have an inkling that this is actually my Jacob moment. You see, while "busy" may not be my MO, being hyper-focused (as most visionaries can be) can keep you so focused on the future that you miss the present circumstance. Boundaries, while preached to be healthy, can also create such a barrier of protection that you restrain the flow of love that is necessary to minister. Ownership then gets shifted back into the hands of the weak, who aren't capable of going it alone.

This is where I found myself. Years before, when my default was to take on other people's problems, to be the hero, mediator, and peacemaker, my therapist suggested I pass the responsibility back to the person who gave it to me. As a result, I became adept at "passing the brick." It was so freeing once I realized I didn't have to people-please or perform. And though relationships no longer require me to carry the baggage (or bricks) of others, they do require that I make space to commune.

Maybe I'm talking in too many hyperboles for you to grasp where I am, where I've been, or even where I'm going. Let me paint a clearer picture. Whether because of the impending death of my father or the impending confinement of my husband, I felt betrayed and helpless. Within a four-day window, my entire life was flipped upside-down. My mind spiraled out, and my body shut down. I was not responding with my typical tendencies of flight or freeze but instead recognized that I had to fight. I had to fight for the life of one and the freedom of the other. And that required an abundance of time, owning my role, and being okay with the mess when it deviated from what my curated "rhythms of grace" usually looked like. This was a new level of pruning I had never faced, and I ran to Jesus to find my refuge.

It sounds like I was making all the right moves. I was surely doing the best I could with what I had, realizing I had zero control in the matter, even though my controls remained intact. I still had my family. I still had my responsibilities as a mama. I still had my friends. I still had my integrity. And most importantly, I still had my Jesus. But as time pressed on and my schedule acclimated to my new roles as nurse and financial manager, I felt less and less capable of sustaining and more and more stuck in the past, the gap, the cyclone of details—the mess rather than the masterpiece of what the clay could produce.

You see, our tendency isn't to release; it's often to manipulate, to self-preserve. I wanted to solve and create security. But what would happen in the depths of my night or my tears was the true telling point of the enemy's strategy to kill, steal, and destroy my very hope and ultimate awareness of safety and comfort. If I trace back the details, then I can understand. If I turn back their stories to the traumas, then I can find a resolution to the predicament we are in. Night by night, overwhelmed, emotional wail by wail, I'd turned into a pillar of salt, like Lot's wife, looking back rather than pressing onward.

Fortunately, my babies, who watched closely as I cried behind my sunglasses or mustered up a happy face for their milestone moments and daily reflection times, kept bringing me back to my present mess and future reality—a reality that was so different from what I had rhythmically avoided and intentionally prepared. This wasn't how it was supposed to be. I had been walking with Jesus so closely. I was doing His work with Him. I was serving His people. I was relishing in our communion as Father and daughter. But I was hyperfocused on what was to come, missing critical moments of discernment that cautioned me to stay rooted in my present life. I missed the warning signs. I avoided tension. I silenced wisdom. I stuffed pain. I made plans. I was intentionally distracted by something good but not fully focused on God in the present. Because, after all, God's got it, right?

You see, life hits us, even when we dwell with Jesus. Unexpected testimony-making moments wreck us, but ultimately, He will remake us. Sanctification, becoming like Jesus and being known by Jesus, isn't a one-off encounter or a good Sunday sermon.

> *And it's the leaning in when nothing makes sense in order to sense His existence in the void of senses.*

It isn't a perfectly constructed masterpiece. It isn't the avoidance of truth to only relish in His Truth. It's the messy middle—the chasm of our temporal existence between this world and heaven. It's the fighting of principalities. It's the wrestling of our bodies, minds, and spirits—our flesh and spirits. And it's the leaning in when nothing makes sense in order to sense His existence in the void of senses. He doesn't run. He positions himself in the sunsets, the calendar invites, the unexpected God winks, the illuminated verses, the highlighted lyrics in worship, and everything in between.

He writes our stories. And while He adores you greatly, He adores all those who are in the muck and mire with you just as much. Their souls have an eternal plan. So, as I process this season, stepping more greatly into my identity as a daughter of the King, I relish in the mess of the making and realize that more than one mosaic piece at a time is likely more than my little heart and mind could handle, anyway. In just a few short weeks, He gave me greater confidence, secured my humble authority, unlocked my voice in areas of deficit, realigned my heart to His perfect will, equipped me with wisdom and counsel, revealed new layers of intimacy in my relationships, and gifted me a holy concern for the condition of the heart without the Holy Spirit. He is shaping me to be more like Him.

You may be baptized. You may lift your hands in worship. You may have wisdom and peace and other portions of the fruits of the Spirit as well. But when you have a hidden pocket, a secret, a vice, or an idol that has crept in as your priority, your focus, or your god, you won't ever grasp the freedom promised on this side of heaven. You can't serve both. He is a jealous God who wants all of you. And He has good, good gifts to bless you with. But spiritual adultery is still infidelity. And your eternity rests in the capable and loving hands of the One who already gave His life for the very thing you cling to as a comfort or "good enough." Nothing is more fulfilling than being naked and unafraid, walking in the cool of the day with your creator who, from the beginning of time, has called you very good.

The messy thing about cheating is the layers of lies that have led you astray, but the beautiful thing about Truth is the healing balm that reveals identity and safety in the One who welcomes you home. As I flew back home from Denver, relishing the intentional time with the Lord, I thanked Him for the ray that revealed my places of bondage—the parts of me still trying to control the outcomes, the parts of me carrying unforgiveness, the parts of me holding onto doubt and the past. And I thanked Him for making me more fully aware of the newest gift (rather than brick), which is the newest mess of my *always-becoming* message. I rest in the certainty that it's not *anything* that's happened *to* me but *everything* that's happened *for* me that will allow me to ultimately expand His kingdom here on Earth and to do so boldly.

So here I am, letting you know the best is yet to come, and your current valley doesn't mean you are far from Jesus; it means you are being perfected from glory to glory. And as goodness and mercy chase you down as promised in Psalm 23, you don't have to fear, for His rod and staff will comfort you. There are streams of living water running through the valley, and He will set a table in the presence of your enemy so you may dine with the exquisite painter of the very sunrises and sunsets that bring you to a pause. Before I knew Jesus like this, I was still His prized possession. Now, I just get to relish in the richer facets of His character and represent Him in a new and profound way.

Christ is gentle.

> "You have given me the shield of your salvation, and your right hand supported me, and your gentleness made me great" (Psalm 18:35, ESV).
>
> "Let your gentleness be evident to all" (Philippians 4:5, NIV).
>
> "Be completely humble and gentle; be patient, bearing with one another in love" (Ephesians 4:2, NIV).

What valley experience or current situation in your life (even if not your "fault") could offer an opportunity for self-reflection to shift your pace, repent through your posture of ownership, adjust your focused perspective on the past versus the future, and give you a newfound passion for people—and ultimately an invitation for becoming more like Jesus?

pray

Reflect

Write

TAMRA ANDRESS is a seven-time best-selling author (and counting), featured in *Forbes*, *USA Today*, and many other well-known publications. She's a keynote speaker and top podcaster for *The Messenger Movement*, *The Flounder Collective Podcast*, and *Girls Gone Holy*. She's a serial entrepreneur who works with high-capacity Christian leaders, mobilizing them to become millionaire messengers and share the Good News. She is wildly in love with words and the Word! Through her publishing company, F.I.T. in Faith Press, she catalyzes messengers in the marketplace by building business as a ministry through publishing, podcasting, and platform development while keeping play at the core! Her nonprofit, The Founder Collective, focuses on ordaining and sustaining marketplace ministers.

Sanctification is the process of removing impurities from an object or person. Unlike purification, it is not a one-time thing but a continual renewing or removal of impurities that occur over time. Sanctification is a gradual deepening of our understanding of Christ and the power we have access to because of who He is, not who we are.

Jori O'Nealle

Chapter 7

Becoming His Disciple
By Jori O'Neale

Sanctification is the process of removing impurities from an object or person. Unlike purification, it is not a one-time thing but a continual renewing or removal of impurities that occurs over time. Sanctification is a gradual deepening of our understanding of Christ and the power we have access to because of who He is, not who we are.

I like to think of sanctification in terms of iron being refined by fire over and over again. This process ensures that impurities are removed and results in a metal strong enough to carry out the purpose for which it was created. Our refining is similar. It takes many forms and is often accompanied by extreme discomfort and even pain. But behind that pain is purpose. Behind the pain of sanctification are hope and power—the hope that we are no longer the same and the power to transform into who God is calling us to be.

I wish I had understood sanctification when I was first introduced to Jesus. I spent many years learning about Him but not really getting to know Him. I found you can be familiar with someone and never truly know them. You can know *about* them but not have a real relationship *with* them. That's how I was raised, learning and having a head knowledge about God and Jesus but never truly learning how to receive the power and authority Jesus promised me in Matthew 28:18–20 (NLT). "Jesus came and told his disciples, 'I have been given all authority in heaven and on earth. Therefore, go and make disciples of all the nations, baptizing them in the name of the Father and the Son and the Holy Spirit. Teach these new disciples to obey all the commands I have given you. And be sure of this: I am with you always, even to the end of the age.'"

Relating to God as my father was difficult because I didn't grow up with my biological father. Even after my mom married my stepdad, the strained relationship between us didn't help my understanding of who God was. I had father figures in my life, but none of them were men I felt safe with, that is until I began attending church. At church, I had "big brothers," "uncles," and even men who had replaced my granddad after his passing. I became immersed in the youth group and participated in all the activities. At twelve, I gave my life to God and got saved. I didn't fully understand what salvation meant, but I saw everyone else in the youth group doing it, so I joined in. After an incident of sexual abuse during a church trip, that all changed. I questioned God's goodness and even His existence. My behavior and mood changed; I fell into depression and rarely wanted to go to church. I felt like Job. It seemed like I was being tested to see if I actually believed the things I said I believed. But unlike Job, I was failing miserably and got involved in activities I knew were not of God.

So, although I knew of Jesus and read the Bible religiously, my heart was far from Him. Paul, the apostle, experienced the same thing. He grew up holding to a very strict law and condemned anyone who fell outside of it—even to death. While I've never physically hurt anyone, my words have wounded many a person. One of my victims came back to share that my torture of her and her character had caused her to attempt self-harm. I was seventeen years old, not even able to vote, but at that moment, I came to the stark realization that words are powerful, so much so that they could take a life. Her next statement blew me away. She said she forgave me and was sorry for whatever hurt I was experiencing that caused me to lash out at her in such a way. Like Paul on the road to Damascus, I was blinded by the love of Jesus and unable to see the damage I was doing to God's people.

After that conversation, I went silent for a while—not for a few moments but for months. Knowing that I had caused a lot of hurt and unforgiveness, I felt the best course of action was just to stop talking altogether so as not to cause further damage or hurt anyone else. The enemy had convinced me that the very thing God had called me to use to share His message was a weapon of mass destruction, one that I needed to stifle.

But then the wildest thing occurred, and no one really seemed to notice—no one except my best friend, Porsche. She and I had been besties since third grade and were now about to graduate from high school together. She was smart, funny, and popular, and her voice . . . what a gift she had. She also went to church but, unlike me, had men and women in her life who were sowing good seeds into her and allowing her to freely use her God-given gifts. Instead of badgering me with questions, she sat silently beside me during lunch and loved me. She didn't desire anything in return; she was just there as a constant reminder of the love of God. It was at that moment that Jesus was making himself known. He was no longer just a man who preachers and pastors spoke about on Sundays or a character in Bible stories. Jesus was real—so real that He rescues people even to this day. He rescued my bullying victim, and her forgiveness was the first catalyst on my road to sanctification. I understood for the first time that being like Jesus had nothing to do with following rules, judging others, or living by a strict moral code. Being like Jesus meant loving like Jesus, forgiving like Jesus, and sharing your gifts freely to promote the name of Jesus.

> *I understood for the first time that being like Jesus had nothing to do with following rules, judging others, or living by a strict moral code.*

"This means that anyone who belongs to Christ has become a new person. The old life is gone; a new life has begun!" (2 Corinthians 5:17, NLT).

The next time I experienced sanctification was probably the hardest. To learn how to truly be like Jesus and grow closer to Him, I left behind my former ways of life and everything familiar to me. In the same year that I experienced the forgiveness of a former friend and the constant love of God from a current one, I was awarded a full-ride scholarship to St. John's University. It was over seven hundred miles and twelve hours away from everyone and everything I had ever known. It was the opportunity of a lifetime and a life-changing one, but my parents were not on board. I knew a decision had to be made. Should I stay in this environment and continue down the same destructive path, or should I go against my parents' wishes and travel across the country to an unfamiliar place without their blessing or support? I had a heart-to-heart with my mother and told her that if she wouldn't help me, I would still go because I really believed leaving home was the only way to save my life. We cried and prayed and hugged, and then we packed her car and left in the night, against my father's wishes. She drove twelve hours to New York, dropped me off at my dorm, helped me make my bed, and drove twelve hours back—no stopping, except for gas. I still have no idea how she did it. But I realized that day that my mother was not to blame for the way my life had turned out, and my forgiveness of her released me to experience the love of God more fully.

> "'Yes,' Jesus replied, 'and I assure you that everyone who has given up house or brothers or sisters or mother or father or children or property, for my sake and for the Good News, will receive now in return a hundred times as many houses, brothers, sisters, mothers, children, and property—along with persecution. And in the world to come that person will have eternal life'"
> (Mark 10:29–30, NLT).

Being away from my family was tough, but God met me in my isolation and sent people to show me the way, just like He sent Ananias to Paul (Acts 9:10–18). I had to release my previous ways of thinking about Jesus and Scripture and become like a child, allowing myself to learn from others and to trust again, which was the hardest part. I was met by a young man in art class and invited to a campus Bible study. After studying the Bible for three weeks, I decided to truly give my life to Jesus, and I was baptized into Christ in March 2002.

About five years after my baptism, the "Paul" in me resurfaced. I started judging others again and holding them to my self-righteous standards. Were they not really Christians? I had become so judgmental that even the ministers at my church took me aside to discuss my pride. Once again, my words were wreaking havoc in the lives of God's people, and instead of building up the house of God, I was tearing it down brick by brick with every word I spoke. I am not proud of how I behaved, but I share this because many of you may be in a similar situation—sitting on the front pew and, at times, on the back pew, sizing up and comparing everyone sitting in between. You may not be as extreme as I was because I tend to have an all-or-nothing type of spirit, but maybe you sit in judgment of others instead of engaging and leaning in with curiosity about who they truly are. You seek to know no more than what you currently do, and although you may not boast about your good works, your refusal to go deeper into the Word of God still emits the same stench of pride.

> *Once again, my words were wreaking havoc in the lives of God's people, and instead of building up the house of God, I was tearing it down brick by brick with every word I spoke.*

As I stated before, sanctification is not a one-time thing. I needed to be renewed daily and strive to go deeper in my relationship with God. This was a step closer to growing into the person God desired me to be. Despite all the good things I was doing, I was no closer to being like Jesus than the day I was baptized. I didn't trust God or His Word in the way I knew I needed to and still harbored feelings of unforgiveness toward so many. After being challenged to forgive like Jesus, I wrote a letter to the deacon of my former church who had molested me, and through a tear-stained piece of paper, I forgave him. I felt an immense weight lift off of me. The burden I was carrying was gone, and it was replaced by God's peace. I felt unstoppable and light, two things I hadn't felt in over a decade. I began to work on my relationship with my biological father, which was still very strained. I used Skype to connect monthly, catch up, and build a friendship. The more I healed from my past trauma and forgave, the closer I felt to God and the more present His Spirit seemed.

One of my greatest trials of sanctification came during the Winter of 2021. I had just had ACL surgery and was lying in my bed, feeling all sorts of pain and sorrow. I'm not talking about godly sorrow that leads to repentance but the world's sorrow that leads to death. I had somehow blamed God for my injury and was now feeling like the same helpless girl I was in high school. After attempting to get something to eat and being unable to hold my crutches and the plate of food, I sat in my bedroom, feeling absolutely defeated. It was at that moment I heard someone say, "Get up." Knowing I was home alone, I was scared and thought I might be going crazy from being isolated all day. "Get up and take up your mat."

I mustered enough courage to ask, "Lord, is that you?"

"Do you want to get well?" He asked.

"Yes, Lord, I want to get well," I said.

"Then, get up!" He thundered.

I grabbed my crutches and stood up. The Lord instructed me to make room for what He was about to do in my life and told me to clean my guest room. With one good leg and a hip brace, I went through the painstaking task of clearing out and cleaning up my guest room. I created a prayer corner that faced a window, put a desk and chair near the door, and placed fresh linens on the guest bed. It was in that room over the next twelve months that the Lord would use me to write three books, start three podcasts, baptize a woman, and begin my weekly habit of live broadcasting sermons and messages of hope via social media.

None of that was on my radar at the end of 2021. Each time I released something to Jesus, He opened a door, and I had the choice to trust and go through or stay and give way to fear. I started attending workshops and online conferences focused on having the mind of Christ and being renewed from the inside out. Romans 12:2 (NLT) says, "Don't copy the behavior and customs of this world, but let God transform you into a new person by changing the way you think. Then you will learn to know God's will for you, which is good and pleasing and perfect." This verse emphasizes the importance of renewing our minds through prayer and studying God's Word to align our thoughts and desires with God's will. This is a teaching that, sadly, many a congregation fail to emphasize. They want the works and good deeds without the renewing of the mind. I believe that if a mind is transformed, a life is set on fire for God. *Sanctification can't work unless you work it.* Once we pray for our minds to be in alignment with the Word of God and put the Scriptures into action, God makes His ways known to us, and we get to walk in boldness, confidence, and abundance, not in fear, timidity, and scarcity.

Because of my life experiences, the character trait of Jesus I strive to imitate the most is *forgiveness*. Forgiveness has saved my life, both as a sinner seeking a savior and as a human with flaws who harms others and experiences harm. Forgiveness transformed my relationship with God and man. The Word of God transforms my mind, and sanctification transforms my life.

What areas of your life need to be transformed
through sanctification?

pray

Reflect

Write

JORI O'NEALE is an author, speaker, and productivity coach passionate about helping others deepen their relationship with God through faith and intentional living. As a co-author of *More Than Enough: The Silent Struggle of a Woman's Identity*, Jori shares her journey of overcoming trauma, finding healing, and discovering her identity in Christ. Her experiences have shaped her commitment to guiding others in their walk with God and helping them uncover the strength that comes through faith and forgiveness.

Through her workshops, which include the "Your Story Matters Writing Workshop" for aspiring authors, the "Your Productivity Matters Coaching Program" for educators, "Empowering Students to Discover Their Gifts," and "Building Identity and Confidence Through Faith" for schools, churches, and faith-based organizations, Jori encourages believers to align their lives with God's purpose. She also hosts the podcast *Thirty Minutes of Power*, where she challenges her listeners to embrace the power God has given them to uplift and empower others. Jori's writings and teachings are a testament to how God can transform pain into purpose, and she is dedicated to inspiring others to pursue a deeper, more intimate relationship with Him.

Sanctification is an exciting adventure with Jesus—a daily invitation to take hold of His hand and, with steps of faith, become the amazing person your heavenly Father created you to be. This process is full of ups and downs, twists and turns, and mountain tops and valleys. Sometimes, it is both exciting and scary, as the details aren't always made clear. Yet, one powerful truth always remains the same: Jesus is always present, always faithful, and always victorious.

Ashley Weston

Chapter 8

The Invitation for More
By Ashley Weston

*S*anctification is an exciting adventure with Jesus—a daily invitation to take hold of His hand and, with steps of faith, become the amazing person your heavenly Father created you to be. This process is full of ups and downs, twists and turns, and mountain tops and valleys. Sometimes, it is both exciting and scary, as the details aren't always made clear. Yet, one powerful truth remains the same: Jesus is always present, always faithful, and always victorious.

Let me tell you about my journey with Jesus. . . .

THE INVITATION TO SURRENDER

Jesus met me on an airplane traveling from Atlanta, Georgia, to Managua, Nicaragua, on January 26, 2006. My parents had invited me to serve with them on a mission trip, sharing the Good News with the people of the remote island of Ometepe. Even though I had been "saved" since I was twelve, read my Bible occasionally, and had gone to church my entire life, going on this mission trip seemed different. God had been working on my heart for the past six months, as I was not content with the way my life was going. Something felt off. I was successful on the outside, but my heart was still empty. So over the course of those six months, I had been trying to "change myself" by training for a marathon and developing a consistent quiet time before each training run to "connect" with Jesus. I was truly *trying* to draw near to Jesus in that process and let go of all the sins I had been tolerating (and also enjoying). So when my parents invited me to go on the mission trip with them, I immediately said yes! I would be serving on the team hosting an evangelist from Argentina named Carlos Annacondia, who would lead a three-night revival event for the people of Ometepe.

As I sat on that plane, intently reading Evangelist Annacondia's book, *Listen to Me, Satan*, I clearly heard Jesus speak to me. He said, "I don't want any of you if I cannot have all of you." My heart started pounding as the fear of God fell upon me; I knew what He was talking about. My version of being a Christian was surrendering to Jesus only the things I wanted to surrender. I was calling Him "Savior," but I had not acknowledged Him as Lord over all. Unfortunately, I was still enjoying living in sin. So, as I heard that hard statement, I quickly realized it was the most loving and kind thing Jesus could have ever said to me. What I would soon find out was that He was inviting me to more—more love, more joy, more freedom, and more of Him. He was inviting me into a divine exchange—giving Him all of my sins, hurt, and pain and receiving something so much better in return!

> *… I clearly heard Jesus speak to me. He said, "I don't want any of you if I cannot have all of you."*

When I got to my hotel room that night, I was ready. I got on my hands and knees, face down to the floor, and wept in His presence. I recalled the hurt and pain from my childhood, along with the many petty sins that were offensive to Him, and I asked Jesus to forgive me. And then I gave it all to Him. I pictured laying it at the foot of the cross and leaving it there.

The next night, as Pastor Annacondia preached the Good News of Jesus to the sea of people in front of him, I witnessed so many hungry souls with desperate hearts for a Savior—a Savior who was all they had yet more than enough. They needed food, clothing, and shelter, but more than that, they needed physical healing. And as I watched with a heart still raw from the night before, the Gospel was preached, and I saw Jehovah Rapha, the Lord my Healer, touch many in the crowd. But they were not the only ones He touched. Since the age of eight, scoliosis had damaged my spine, causing lower back pain. But that night, as my heart was moved by the spoken Word and the sight of people hungry for a miraculous touch from Jesus, He touched my back and radically healed me. He not only took away my heart pain but also my physical pain. And with this amazing, divine exchange, He also gave me joy where there had been sadness. With surprise, I realized He didn't want anything from me; He wanted so much more for me . . . and so the journey began.

When I returned home, I wasn't the same person who had left. My eyes were opened, and my big dreams for the future were now completely changed. I didn't want to pursue success anymore, only Him. I wanted more of Jesus. As exciting as this was, it was also very confusing because the path I had mapped out for myself was now unappealing. So, as I prayed, I told the Lord I wanted to quit my nine-to-five job and serve Him fully. I didn't know what that looked like, but I knew I didn't want to be where I was anymore. Despite how I felt, Jesus told me to wait. He specifically told me to wait seven years, just like Jacob waited for Rachel in Genesis 29. As hard as it was to receive that direction from the Lord, I chose to submit and wait.

THE INVITATION TO WAIT AND BE PREPARED

After choosing to obey Jesus, adventure and excitement were the fruit of submission. Yes, at times, it was hard. Actually, it was very hard, and I struggled with not understanding why I had to wait, why I couldn't be with my precious children every day, and why I couldn't serve Him in ministry full-time. But God was faithful every step of the way. I returned to Nicaragua each January with my family and church and continued to see Jesus, the Great Physician, show up and perform many miracles. Through the laying on of hands and prayers led by the Holy Spirit, I witnessed Jesus heal the sick, give sight to the blind, and make the lame walk, along with many other miracles.

Jesus constantly invited me to step into more divine exchanges. He helped me give Him selfishness for servanthood. He faithfully grew me out of immaturity to rest fully in Him.

He asked me to give Him many worldly things that were good but not His best for me. And though I didn't always understand His reasons, I obeyed because I trusted Him. It wasn't always easy, and I wasn't always eager to give Him what He asked of me, but I did, and He blessed me for trusting Him.

Even though it wasn't my choice to stay in my nine-to-five desk job, it proved to be the perfect preparation for the promised land He had prepared for me. Jesus sent people into my workplace and showed me how to evangelize to them. He prompted me to pray for them in a corporate setting, even though it wasn't normal or comfortable. He placed me in a position of leadership and taught me how to run a business and manage people. Jesus held my hand every step of the way because He is the Good Shepherd. It was a hard seven years because my flesh hated waiting, but it was also wonderful because Jesus was truly present and teaching me so many things!

THE INVITATION TO ENTER THE PROMISED LAND

When the seven years had passed, I knew Jesus was inviting me to follow Him somewhere new. Honestly, I thought Jesus would reveal more of the details to make the leap of faith easier, but He didn't. I just knew a promised land was ahead, and I could either choose to stay where I was (which gave me a sense of security) or take a leap of faith, holding His hand and venturing into an unknown land filled with possibilities! It seemed as if I was being shown the same picture as Joshua, a promised land full of giants, and God was asking me to trust Him and to go anyway because He was with me! And so I went!

I left my job, with all of its perks, benefits, and big salary, and followed Jesus. I didn't know what He was inviting me to, but I was trusting He would provide for my family's needs. I gave Him my financial security, and He showed me that He was my provider, not my job. In the days that followed, when worry tried to creep in and funds became low, I would stop, pray, and declare His promises over me and trust in them. Jesus came through every time, and there was always more than enough.

Six months after taking the leap of faith, Jesus showed me a glimpse of the promised land He was calling me to enter. My mom came over one day to "play" and be creative. She brought with her some jewelry-making supplies. While molding a clay medallion for my first necklace, I heard Jesus whisper, "Make a necklace for yourself, write your life verse on the back, and wear it." And so, I did just that. I made a pretty circular medallion and wrote Proverbs 3:5 (NIV) on the back: "Trust in the Lord with all your heart and lean not on your own understanding." The necklace turned out beautifully, and as I wore it each day, it became a reminder to talk to Jesus whenever my heart wanted to give in to worry or fear. It became another invitation to believe in His promises for me instead of in what I physically saw before me. Jesus was again in pursuit of more divine exchanges, moving me from worry to trust, from doubt to belief, and from seeking others to seeking Him first.

Over the next few months, I made more necklaces. I really enjoyed selecting unique stones and creating different crosses to adorn them. I also had fun talking to Jesus about which Bible verses to inscribe on the backs of the medallions that might be helpful for the wearer. I would stay up late making jewelry while listening to sermons or worship songs. As I began telling friends about the jewelry I was creating (or what Jesus had inspired me to create), people became curious and wanted to purchase some of my pieces. Before my first customer arrived, I heard Jesus whisper, "Ashley, I want you to pray over every person who purchases jewelry." Excited, I said yes to Jesus. When it came time for my friend to purchase, I got nervous. But as she was walking out the door, I felt Jesus nudge me, reminding me of my promise to Him. Surrendering my fear of man, I asked my friend if I could pray for her, and she agreed, even though she was hesitant and a little weirded out. As I prayed, Jesus did something new in me! He poured forth from my mouth His powerful love, acceptance, and concern for my friend. Those words touched her heart to receive His love for the first time. As she left, holding the two necklaces in her hands, she also took with her my sweet Jesus and His love in her heart.

After that encounter with Jesus, I knew that this was what He had been preparing me for. The next day, as I spent time with Him in worship and reading the Bible, He opened my eyes while in the book of Colossians, and I heard Him whisper the name of the business He was birthing, a business all about Him: Hidden Truth Jewelry. Yet another invitation . . .

The past nine years of ministering in the marketplace, making jewelry, praying for others, and, most importantly, sharing my sweet Jesus with everyone I meet have truly been the most amazing adventure I could have ever dreamed of. But even though I have been living in my "promised land," there have been many giants to fight along the way. God told Joshua, "Have I not commanded you? Be strong and courageous. Do not be afraid; do not be discouraged, for the LORD your God will be with you wherever you go" (Joshua 1:9, NIV). And just as He was with Joshua, God has been faithful to be with me wherever I have gone and to give me victory. He has helped me destroy the giant of greed by inviting me to be spontaneously generous with customers and allowing me to witness a revival of faith as I am obedient to that call. He has enabled me to destroy the orphan spirit that lied to me about who I was, thus helping me live confidently as a beloved daughter of God. Jesus has taught me to walk by faith, and I have learned to dance with Him, sometimes pivoting suddenly without understanding but always with trust. After seeing countless miracles, signs, and wonders and the fulfillment of His Word coming to pass, He has helped me destroy the giant of doubt and unbelief. Jesus has been present with me in the waiting rooms of life, in the loneliness, in the hurt, in the pain, and in the suffering, all while providing constant joy, peace, and hope—I have learned that's who He is. Knowing Jesus has been the best journey I could have ever chosen, and I am excited each and every new day—no matter what it holds—because I know He will be with me!

> *Jesus has been present with me in the waiting rooms of life, in the loneliness, in the hurt, in the pain, and in the suffering, all while providing constant joy, peace, and hope*

Matthew 28:18–20 (NIV) says, "Then Jesus came to them and said, 'All authority in heaven and on earth has been given to me. Therefore go and make disciples of all nations, baptizing them in the name of the Father and of the Son and of the Holy Spirit, and teaching them to obey everything I have commanded you. And surely I am with you always, to the very end of the age.'"

The one defining quality of Jesus that has helped me, changed me, and spurred me on since my powerful encounter with Him in 2006 is *His powerful presence.*

What is Jesus inviting you into right now? Do you need to surrender all? Lay it down and receive the divine exchange He has for you. Is Jesus inviting you to wait and prepare for who He created you to become? Abide in Him and wait for Him to lead you each step of the way. Or are you standing on the edge of your promised land, like Joshua, and Jesus is nudging you to take that leap of faith, even amid the giants you see ahead? Then, take the leap, face the fear, let go, and trust that Jesus is present with you. The giants will be defeated, and your promised land is waiting.

No matter where you are, Jesus is present and inviting you to more. Trust Him. He will always give you victory because He is victory. He will work it all together for good as you keep your eyes on Him and love Him (Romans 8:28). And He will give you exceedingly abundantly more than all you could ever ask or imagine (Ephesians 3:20). That's who He is!

Take a moment, close your eyes, and picture Jesus right in front of you. He has so much more for you, friend. Are you ready to receive it?

What is the invitation Jesus is holding out
for you right now?

pray

Reflect

Write

ASHLEY WESTON, a.k.a. the Jesus cheerleader, is super passionate about sharing the *joy* of the Lord with everyone she meets! She is a wife of twenty-three years, a mother to two amazing kids, and the founder of Hidden Truth Jewelry, a jewelry line that clothes women with God's powerful Word. In addition, Ashley is the author of the best-selling art-devotional book *I Am Who You Say I Am*, written to remind women of their identity as God's beloved daughters, and she is a co-author of the Amazon best-seller *The Joy-Full Entrepreneur: Awaken, Renew, Transform*. Ashley loves spurring on women of all ages and stages, reminding them of the amazing adventure Jesus offers in an intimate relationship. Ashley is so passionate about sharing the hope of Jesus with people because He radically changed her life and miraculously healed her of scoliosis in 2006. She wants people everywhere to experience the same tender yet powerful touch of the Lord!

"When I Pray, 'Lord, show me what sanctification means for me', He will show me. It means being made one with Jesus. Sanctification is not something Jesus puts in me—it is Himself in me (1 Corinthians 1:30)." —Oswald Chambers, My Utmost for His Highest (emphasis added)

April Foster

Chapter 9

The Journey to Trust Jesus for Our Loved Ones

By April Foster

"When I pray, 'Lord, show me what *sanctification* means for me,' He will show me. *It means being made one with Jesus.* Sanctification is not something Jesus puts in me—it is *Himself* in me (1 Corinthians 1:30)."
—Oswald Chambers, *My Utmost for His Highest* (emphasis added)

A few years ago, I watched a video of birds hatching from their eggs. Interestingly, I discovered it can take days for them to break free. The mother bird watches nearby, never helping crack the egg from the outside. The baby birds squawk loudly, crying for their mother to help them escape. But if the mother helped them, their wings wouldn't be strong enough for them to survive. In the struggle came the strength.

I have struggled to see myself as valuable and believed the lie that I was insignificant. I lived a life of performance and perfection, hoping it would fill my longing to be seen and valued. Deep in the core of my soul, I desired to be saved from myself. I felt like a baby bird—alone, helpless, and crying out in the darkness.

Jesus promised never to leave us, but He also said we would struggle. Not once did Jesus ever leave me. Why? Because He promised. Yet, at times, I doubted and still doubt. This is how the journey of sanctification can feel, and just like with the baby birds, it can be a struggle that takes time.

There are two parts to a surrender: Savior and Lord. The sanctification process requires total surrender to both parts. Because of deep-rooted trust issues, allowing Jesus to be Lord over my life was not easy. Time after time, circumstance upon circumstance, my obedience in following Him where He led proved Him trustworthy. Every time I yielded, I was becoming more like Him. The more I permitted Him to reside in me, the less I ruled and reigned.

It was one thing to believe and trust Jesus for myself, but trusting Him for the salvation of my loved ones was totally different. Sometimes, I was tempted to scream at them to wake up and see God's goodness. I had forgotten so quickly that there was a time in my life when I couldn't see His goodness either. It takes faith to believe. It requires trust to walk by faith and not by sight (2 Corinthians 5:7).

In 2017, I entered unfamiliar territory that required a different level of trust. In obedience to God, our children were homeschooled through high school and deeply rooted in His Word. My oldest daughter had turned eighteen and was heading off to college. Before she left, our family took a trip to Heber Springs, Arkansas. Through a divine appointment, a man named Coach led us on a hike up Sugarloaf Mountain. Climbing Sugarloaf and watching my children take risks as they navigated the sharp, steep rocks caused a deep fear to rise within me. At times, I had to look away and trust that Coach would guide us to safety.

I remember freaking out so many times as I watched my kids take those risks I never thought they would take. Once I got to the top of the mountain, I had a serious talk with God. I remember hearing a still, small voice in the mountaintop winds saying, "Do you trust me?"

"Yes, I trust you," I responded.

I heard the question again, but I perceived it differently this time. "Do you trust me with your children?" My answer didn't come as quickly. I cried a deep cry from the depths of my being, realizing that I trusted God but not with my children. I repented at the top of Sugarloaf that day and asked Jesus to help me let go of control and trust Him with my children. That moment helped me realize how tightly I held both of them. I wanted to save them. I didn't want them to struggle. I didn't want to see them get hurt. The Lord asked me to unclench my fists from their fighting posture, open palms of praise, and trust Him. And just as I struggled, so would my children. Just like my journey, my children wouldn't be exempt from pain or suffering. He reminded me to give them grace and space. In the struggle comes strength.

On that beautiful mountaintop morning, I eventually said yes to trusting the Holy Trinity team to lead, love, and launch my children. The Lord reminded me He loved them more than I could ever love them. He reminded me of His goodness and faithfulness. He reminded me I must walk by faith and not by sight (2 Corinthians 5:7). Faith is the substance of what we hope for and the assurance of what is unseen (Hebrews 11:1). I can't see my children's futures, but I am connected to the One who can. He is trustworthy.

Over the past seven years, I have witnessed my children adulting. Both of them successfully left the nest with a grounded foundation in the Word of God. I sat back and watched, yielding to the One who created them and knew every hair on their heads. My husband and I were their shepherds until it was time for "the Shepherd" to lead them.

I witnessed my daughter turn away from knowing God to knowing the world. I heard her tell me she didn't have a mustard seed of faith. She didn't want to hear or talk about Scripture anymore. I witnessed my son turn away from church because he was deceived and led by a false shepherd. His heart hardened with unforgiveness. Each turn shook my heart.

Injustice always fills me with rage. This was an injustice! I wanted to be angry and take control. I wanted to blame someone for this, and I no longer wanted to trust Jesus to handle it. I followed the template, raising our children in God's Word in a loving, supportive home, surrounded by a community of like-minded believers. I gave control to Jesus on that mountain. What did I do wrong? Why wasn't He saving them?

The Holy Spirit reminded me that *love always wins*. I quieted my body, closed my eyes, and took deep breaths. I asked Jesus to open the eyes of my heart. I leaned into Him, just like John, the disciple Jesus loved. I rested my head on Jesus's chest and felt His heartbeat. He reminded me that the beat of His heart not only throbbed for me but also for my children. If He could save me, He could save them. He is trustworthy.

> *The Holy Spirit reminded me that love always wins.*

Jesus urged me to journal what it means to love my children unconditionally. As I wrote, I felt the Holy Spirit writing through me. I opened The Passion Translation Bible (TPT) to 1 Corinthians 13, where love is defined. The thoughts and feelings in my mind and heart could not be expressed, but the Holy Spirit translated them for me.

"If I were to speak with eloquence in earth's many languages, and in the heavenly tongues of angels, yet I didn't express myself with love, my words would be reduced to the hollow sound of nothing more than a clanging cymbal" (1 Corinthians 13:1, TPT).

This verse's commentary states: "The Aramaic word for love is *hooba*, and it is a homonym that also means 'to set on fire.' It is difficult to fully express the meaning of this word and translate it into English. You could say the Aramaic concept is 'burning love' or 'fiery love,' coming from the inner depths of the heart as an eternal energy, an active power of bonding hearts and lives in secure relationships. The Greek word is *agape*, which describes the highest form of love. It is the love God has for his people. It is an intense affection that must be demonstrated. It is a loyal, endless, and unconditional commitment of love. Feelings are attached to this love. It is not abstract, but devoted to demonstrating the inward feelings of love toward another with acts of kindness and benevolence."

My love for each of my children was carefully knit together when my womb became their first home. Because God knew them before I knew them, He is credited with loving them first. I will never be able to give them the perfect love they deserve on this side of heaven, but He is able. Because of God's perfect love that lives inside of me, I can be His vessel to demonstrate His love for them.

> *I will never be able to give them the perfect love they deserve on this side of heaven, but He is able.*

As I continued to read and journal about this great love, I paused and meditated on several verses in the same chapter. "Love is large and incredibly patient. Love is gentle and consistently kind to all. It refuses to be jealous when blessing comes to someone else. Love does not brag about one's achievements nor inflate its own importance. Love does not traffic in shame and disrespect, nor selfishly seek its own honor. Love is not easily irritated or quick to take offense. Love joyfully celebrates honesty and finds no delight in what is wrong. Love is a safe place of shelter, for it never stops believing the best for others. Love never takes failure as defeat, for it never gives up" (1 Corinthians 13:4–7, TPT).

I had always told my children that my love for them was unconditional. My words were now being tested. Was I going to be able to love them like the words described? I wrestled with the impossibility. Through my sanctification journey of performance and perfection, God revealed my pride for and through my children, which was demonstrated through my desire for them to perform and be perfect. He flipped the script and asked me to apply the same grace that was applied to me. When trusting others for Jesus, we love in the waiting.

I recently wrote a letter to my daughter to bring awareness to my sanctification journey.

Dear Daughter,

As each of us enters a new chapter, having grace for each other is imperative to rebuilding and restoring our relationship. I am learning how to apply grace not only to others but also to myself. I am far from perfect! To be completely transparent, I have been working on myself a lot in this new season of motherhood with adult children, surrendering and yielding to the Spirit of the Lord. For years, I was learning how to be a nurturing and caring mother to you as you grew from a baby to a toddler and then to a middle schooler, a teenager, and an adult. Whenever I thought I understood my role as your mother, I had to shift and learn a new one.

I know I have failed you more times than I can count. Yet, you still love me. I know I have misunderstood you more times than I can count. Yet, you still want me to understand you. Thank you for never giving up on us. Thank you for your forgiveness every time I hurt you. Thank you for your grace every time I asked or didn't ask for it.

Just as you are worthy of love, so am I. Just as you are enough exactly as you are, so am I. Aren't we all worthy of those things, to be loved and accepted for who we are? That is why Jesus came. That is why Mary Magdalene was delivered from the seven demons that plagued her. That is why Jesus chose to reveal himself to the world through a woman at the well who lived with a man and had several husbands before him. That is why His generational line was tainted with a prostitute. He came to prove that we are worthy and loved no matter our shortcomings or lineage. We don't get to choose when we are born or who our mother will be.

We do get to choose how we live our lives. At thirty-three years old, I chose to live my life differently. I chose to follow Jesus. For seventeen years, I have remained loyal to His teachings. I read them daily to remind myself how to live in this world. I am still learning and putting my faith to work. This path has prepared me and equips me daily to handle what I can't. I confess I can't handle what gets thrown at me most days, but He can and does. It can be hard to understand another person's journey unless you have walked in their shoes. I haven't walked in yours, and you haven't walked in mine. That is when compassion and empathy come alive. We can only imagine what someone has been through and can only feel perceived pain. If there is any person on Earth I feel compassion and empathy for, it is you. There isn't another person on this Earth I've cried with and cried for more than you.

There is no other bond on this earth like that of a mother and her daughter. We were connected through an umbilical cord, sharing every part of each other. When you were born, the cord was cut, which began the process of disconnecting from each other. Although we disconnected from the physical cord, we maintained the connection with the intimacy of nursing at my breasts. I believe God created it that way so the disconnect would be gradual. The chasm of physical distance grew as time continued, yet the bond in the spirit remained. I remain in you, and you remain in me. This is a beautiful example of how Jesus remains in the Father and the Father remains in Him. We were always designed to stay connected in the Spirit. I see you, daughter, in the spirit realm. I see us together, laughing and loving each other at a level that will never be possible on this earth. The Earth blocks us (Read more about the new Earth in Isaiah 65:17–25, TPT).

Love, Mom

Unconditional love is essential as we trust Jesus to work in the lives of others. God's Word encourages us to "Watch over each other to make sure that no one misses the revelation of God's grace. And make sure no one lives with a root of bitterness sprouting within them which will only cause trouble and poison the hearts of many" (Hebrews 12:15, TPT). Part of the sanctification journey requires that we not be a stumbling block for the salvation journeys of others. Writing a letter to my daughter helped my heart remain softened and the doors open in our relationship. Think of the baby bird whose strength came through its struggle to break free. The mother bird was there, waiting. Similarly, when our loved ones find freedom in Christ, we should be ready to welcome them with open arms.

> *Unconditional love is essential as we trust Jesus to work in the lives of others.*

"Now may the God of peace himself sanctify you completely, and may your whole spirit and soul and body be kept blameless at the coming of our Lord Jesus Christ. He who calls you is faithful; he will surely do it"
(1 Thessalonians 5:23–24, ESV).

Jesus is trustworthy.

Who is Jesus asking you to surrender and entrust to Him their salvation?

pray

Reflect

Write

APRIL FOSTER is a woman of great influence and purpose. She is a devoted daughter of the Most High King, wife to John for twenty-nine years, and proud mother of two exceptionally talented and driven adult children. April embodies ambition and success, traits she has passed down to her children. She is the founder of a longstanding business, Fostering Foundations, and serves as the area coordinator for T.R.A.C. Life, a national mentoring initiative supporting teenagers in foster care.

April's passion for education led her to homeschool her children through high school, inspiring her to establish Christian classical homeschool communities throughout southeastern Louisiana. Her pioneering spirit not only ensured her own children's academic success but also equipped and encouraged thousands of other families to pursue classical education.

With a Bachelor's Degree in Psychology and a Master's Degree in Counseling, April is dedicated to rebuilding marriages, strengthening families, and helping individuals reclaim their identity in Christ. As an encounter coach, retreat speaker, and host, she provides transformative experiences that resonate deeply. Her podcast, *Bedroom and Bible*, addresses intimate and challenging topics, fostering open, meaningful conversations. As a sought-after trainer and conference speaker, she leaves a powerful and lasting impression on her audiences.

April's career includes leading a successful direct sales business for ten years as a top performer as well as managing communications in the marketing department for a global homeschool company. She has also taught at the collegiate level as a professor, guiding young adults in career development and life skills, and has worked as a job coach for adults with developmental disabilities.

An accomplished author and seed mogul, April has contributed to the Amazon best-seller *The Joy-Full Entrepreneur: Awaken, Renew, Transform* and the anthology *Joyous Journey of Loss*. She has also written her first children's book, *The Unexpected Guest*. Her articles and blogs have been featured in *Classical Conversations* and *The Old Schoolhouse* magazine. Her next book project, *Love Colored the Way*, will be released in Fall 2025.

Allowing the Holy Spirit complete autonomy involves surrendering to His work in order to remove everything that is not reflective of Christ. This process of sanctification purifies our minds and souls, requiring us to submit to His transformative power and actively engage in the crucifixion of lies and beliefs that have kept us enslaved to darkness—ultimately leading to spiritual freedom and alignment with God's truth.

Amber Love

Chapter 10

A New Name
By Amber Love

Allowing the Holy Spirit complete autonomy involves surrendering to His work in order to remove everything not reflective of Christ. This process of *sanctification* purifies our minds and souls, requiring us to submit to His transformative power and actively engage in the crucifixion of lies and beliefs that have kept us enslaved to darkness—ultimately leading to spiritual freedom and alignment with God's truth.

After ten long days in the trauma unit of the Washington Center for Psychoanalysis, I left against their recommendation and climbed into an Uber that took me back home. As we drove, I contemplated what I was going home to. My husband was deployed, and my son was in the care of my sister until I returned. So I was left with my memories—memories of childhood sexual abuse; sex trafficking at the hands of men, who took advantage of my vulnerabilities; drug addiction that started at age eighteen, when I found myself homeless; spiritual abuse from a Christ-centered recovery program; additional sexual assaults into my young adult years; and the vivid memories of a recent assault by someone in the Navy. Although I had responsibilities at home, I wasn't sure I had any strength left to live—for them or for me. I was dead inside.

A few weeks later, I decided I could no longer believe in a God who would allow a lifetime of trauma to continue. Determined to denounce God publicly, I pulled myself together one Sunday and headed to a random church. Finding my way into the sanctuary, I slouched in the back row, taking in all the lights, music, families, and people embracing one another. That was a life not meant for me. I looked up and said, "All right, *God*," with the attitude of a teenager. "You have forty-five minutes or else." Looking back, I realize I was desperate for God to show up as a miracle worker, and He did just that. Unaffected by my attitude, which arose from a place of pain, He showed me mercy and grace.

That morning's service was on Ezekiel and the dry bones and how God brought a dead army to life and defeated the enemy. I was dead, and my bones were dry. *I won't denounce you today but probably tomorrow,* I thought. As I tried to make a quick escape, a couple stopped me, and the man exclaimed, "Hey! You're new here!" I agreed begrudgingly, knowing I was inviting further conversation. "You should come to my wife's Bible study on Monday!" he shared excitedly.

Shocked at her husband's out-of-the-ordinary behavior, his wife told me, "Oh my gosh, you can go to anyone's Bible study; it doesn't have to be mine." Her husband, not following her lead, insisted that I come to hers.

I finally offered, "Hey man, if I agree to go to your wife's Bible study, can I go get some lunch?" He agreed with a smile, and I quickly walked out the church doors.

Upon finding safety in the privacy of my car, I decided to turn my radio to the K-Love station. As if on assignment from God, the words from Lauren Daigle's new song "Come Alive" rang into my soul. No amount of resistance could have

> *"I have nothing to give you," and the Holy Spirit responded, "Give me your nothing."*

kept my tears from staining my white Sunday shirt. I found myself sitting in my pain and crying to the Lord. I was so tired of fighting this life in my own strength. I finally said, "I have nothing to give you," and the Holy Spirit responded, "Give me your nothing." I wish I could say this was the moment I surrendered and never looked back, but even after this amazing encounter of being seen by the Lord, I wasn't ready to trust what I had left of a life to Him.

A New Name

Monday morning came, and I forced myself to get out of bed and head back to the church. A large group of women had gathered, and their laughter and chatter filled the church foyer. I found a seat and quickly began to judge them. *I'm going to tell all these women in their perfect tea-party dresses, with their two and a half children, what I've been through. They'll judge me, and that will be my reason to denounce God,* I thought. With all the strength I had left in me, I interrupted the study conversation, and my pain poured out as I shared my story. I dissociated and was no longer aware of my surroundings, what I was saying, or the agony I was unleashing. As I regained my senses, reorienting with my surroundings, my sight returned first. To my shock, there was no one sitting at the table. For a moment, the pain of their leaving struck harder than I expected. Slowly, my hearing returned, and unidentifiable sounds came from behind me. It was the women. They were praying over me with outstretched hands as if in a battle I couldn't fight alone. One in particular, a four-foot, eleven-inch woman with long, wild blonde hair, declared, "I see you as a child dancing before the Lord, and you will dance again! I see you standing on a stage with a mic, and you are smiling!" Her words rang out a truth I couldn't understand. I knew nothing of what they meant to me or my future and nothing of how they would come to pass.

Looking back, I realize this was the first prophetic word spoken over me. Her words communicated life, hope, and a future. That was the day I surrendered my will to the Lord, the day I gave Him my nothing and allowed Him to bring my dry bones to life. Over

> *He died as though He were a sinner so we could live as though we were not.*

the next year, these women held my hand as I crawled out of Sheol, the place of the dead. I believe Sheol is where the enemy holds those he *thinks* he has overcome and stolen from the Lord. Jesus is not afraid of hell, your darkness, your pain, or your sins. He already overcame the world when He took on our sins as His own—when He died as though He were a sinner so we could live as though we were not. This is mercy, my friends.

Romans 8:28 (NIV) says, "And we know that in all things God works for the good of those who love him, who have been called according to his purpose." I struggled with this verse in the early years of my transformation, as I still didn't understand its meaning or if people really knew what they were saying to me when they quoted it. My heart often responded, "*You* be abused sexually, spiritually, and mentally for your whole life and see if that verse makes you feel better." However, as my walk with the Lord grew, He began to transform my mind and spirit, and I saw this verse come to life. I saw how He would use all my shame, guilt, pain, anger, and hate for the good of others. But it wasn't the feelings He used; it was my transformation from them. Revelation 12:11 (NLT) says, "And they have defeated him by the blood of the Lamb and by their testimony. And they did not love their lives so much that they were afraid to die." Ultimately, these two verses are what wake me up each day and inspire me to share my testimony.

When people come to the Lord, they often think their lives will immediately get better. This is probably because, like with me, life felt like it couldn't get worse. While there is new life and new hope for the future, I discovered this—surrendering to Jesus—is when the real work begins. Here is the good news: life with Christ is hard, but His power lives in you and helps you overcome every evil thing! The very power of God that spoke creation into existence and brought life into our bodies *lives in you*! Now it's time to let the Holy Spirit clean your house and eliminate everything that is not like Him as you pursue holiness. This is sanctification or, as I refer to it, the "purging." Your body is the temple of the Holy Spirit. First Corinthians 6:19 (TPT) says, "Have you forgotten that your body is now the sacred temple of the Spirit of Holiness, who lives in you? You don't belong to yourself any longer, for the gift of God, the Holy Spirit, lives inside your sanctuary."

After years of sexual trauma, it should come as no surprise that I struggled with sexual immorality inside and outside of my marriages. Sex had been redefined by my life traumas and had become the fix I used to avoid negative emotions. It was a vicious cycle that cost me my marriage and forced my child to grow up in a split-family environment. When COVID-19 hit, I was newly separated from my husband and working in the field of crisis intervention, supporting survivors of sex trafficking. My ex and I had decided my son should stay at his home for safety reasons, as my job required me to work with the public. As the coronavirus locked down the world, I was separated from my son for eight weeks. That time apart from him was brutal, and my suffering was compounded by my isolation from the outside world, my work office, my recovery community, and my church. I once again sought relationships to fill this void and found myself surviving COVID-19 with online dating sites, returning to the behaviors that no longer served me in Christ. Feeling emptier and emptier after each encounter, I finally recognized the pattern that was keeping me a slave to this crazy cycle: (1) experience a negative emotion, (2) engage in meaningless sex, (3) feel better in the moment, (4) spiral into depression for two to three days, and repeat—all while trying to maintain a professional job. Again, not surprisingly, this addiction spiraled out of control until I lost my job because of my inability to show up and complete my work. Loss after loss—how long would I continue to do the same thing over and over again while expecting a different result?

The intentional search for freedom began as my desperation increased. Reaching out to my nonbelieving friends, I asked for help, explaining that I had a problem and couldn't stop. They responded, "Girl, just wrap it and be safe!" I don't think they understood I did not have the ability to make safe decisions when it came to my sexual encounters.

Next, I called a sex addiction hotline. *Surely they can help me,* I thought. Yet, they rejected my application, stating, "Women can't have sexual addictions." In what I thought was my last-ditch effort, I asked people who I believed were Christians for help, and their response was, "Amber, God understands you have needs; you'll be fine." I was so disappointed and pretty sure they were wrong and the Bible was clear on sexual relationships outside of marriage. However, I decided not to look it up because then I would be responsible for the information, and I didn't have the strength to make the change on my own.

I think it's important to note that even in this obvious relapse, I was still seeking the Lord, praying, and worshiping in song daily (between the rap songs that validated my worldly choices). Deciding to follow Jesus doesn't mean you wake up the next day free from a lifetime of bad habits. In 2 Corinthians 12:9 (NIV), He says, "My grace is sufficient for you, for my power is made perfect in weakness." As I struggled daily to set boundaries with men to avoid situations that led to intercourse, I found myself on a different type of cycle—a few days (maybe even a week or two) of success that were followed by a brief relapse. This went on for months.

During one of these relapses, I purchased a Bible. Excited when it arrived, I opened it for the first time, and for the next month and a half, it seemed I couldn't open it without reading about sexual immorality and the reasons God tells us to run from it. As I read, I heard God's desire to protect us from grief, heartbreak, and the pain that is passed on to future generations. One Scripture urged me to fight this stronghold in the Spirit and not by my own strength (Zechariah 4:6, NIV). Proverbs 2:16–18 (TPT) says, "Only wisdom can save you from the flattery of the promiscuous woman. . . .You'll find her house on the road to hell." I knew at that moment that I was on that road and had an opportunity to get off—but it was the last exit before the toll.

> ... *"You'll find her house on the road to hell."*

Evening came, and as I sat on my couch, holding my Bible close to my chest, I rocked back and forth and resisted the urge to "go out." "In my weakness, He is strong" (2 Corinthians 12:9), I repeated to myself as I watched the time pass, with minutes feeling like hours and hours like days. I made it through that evening, but I will never forget what it felt like to deny myself and choose to trust God for healing and freedom.

That experience now brings me comfort as God continues to sift me in the sanctification process. Whose strength carries you as you run the race toward holiness? Will you allow God's boundless power to influence your journey? Sisters, I encourage you to press *into* the pain; don't run from it. Allow the Holy Spirit's fire to consume everything unlike Him until it doesn't even seem like a sacrifice anymore.

> "Rivers of pain and persecution will never extinguish this flame. Endless floods will be unable to quench this raging fire that burns within you. Everything will be consumed. It will stop at nothing as you yield everything to this furious fire until it won't even seem to you like a sacrifice anymore" (Song of Songs 8:7, TPT).

In Christ's letters to the church, Revelation 2 is full of beautiful promises for those who overcome and are victorious. Revelation 2:12–17 (TPT) specifically gave me the courage to continue in my race to holiness. For those who are victorious against sexual immorality, Jesus said, "I will let him feast on the hidden manna and give him a shining white stone. And written upon the white stone is inscribed his new name, known only to the one who receives it." Hallelujah! I will be known not by the name I have carried on Earth but by a new name given to me by the One who knows my innermost thoughts and created me before the foundations of the earth were laid (Ephesians 1:4)!

As I meditated on Jesus's words, I lightheartedly told my therapist, "But I want a new name now!" He laughed and told me I'd have to wait. "Why?" I responded. I have spent my entire life becoming who people needed me to be to obtain their love, and God *is* love. With this new understanding, I went to the courthouse and took my Father's name, "Love." Changing my name didn't remove the memories or the consequences of the decisions I had made in life, but it does remind me to Whom I belong as I continue to run my race toward holiness. What name will be engraved on the white stone God places in your hand, symbolizing your victory over sin and transformation in Christ? Could this new identity shape the way you live today?

Christ is love.

> "For the greatest love of all is a love that sacrifices all. And this great love is demonstrated when a person sacrifices his life for his friends" (John 15:13, TPT).

> "But Christ proved God's passionate love for us by dying in our place while we were still lost and ungodly!" (Romans 5:8, TPT).

"This is love: He loved us long before we loved him. It was his love, not ours. He proved it by sending his Son to be the pleasing sacrificial offering to take away our sins" (1 John 4:10, TPT).

What is God gently asking you to release, deny, or surrender for the sake of drawing closer to Him that is now hindering your spiritual growth, and even in the painful death of your old self, will you trust God fully as you let go of your past identity and embrace new life in Christ?

pray

Reflect

Write

AMBER LOVE, a third-generation survivor of sex trafficking and sexual trauma, transforms her personal journey into a beacon of hope and empowerment for others. Her powerful testimony has been featured on the Christian Broadcasting Network and in the US Navy's revised Sexual Assault Prevention and Response training. Amber mentors survivors and speaks on stages, addressing the effects of sexual trauma and a life of freedom. She co-authored the *God's Heart to Eradicate Trafficking* workbook and recently launched her podcast *Above Zero*. She has also shared her story on podcasts, like David Pasqualone's *Remarkable People Podcast*, *Persons With Lived Experience*, and *Love & Beloved*.

Sanctification is the ongoing journey after coming to faith through which we are gradually transformed to reflect the character, values, and behavior that align more closely with a holy and moral life. It's like growing spiritually, where old, harmful habits and mindsets are slowly replaced by virtues and a deeper relationship with Christ.

Christina Blincoe

Chapter 11

Living in the Truth of His Love

By Christina Blincoe

I was recently introduced to the word *sanctification*. Sanctification is the ongoing journey after coming to faith through which we are gradually transformed to reflect the character, values, and behavior that align more closely with a holy and moral life. It's like growing spiritually, where old, harmful habits and mindsets are slowly replaced by virtues and a deeper relationship with Christ.

I am here with you today to share my real and raw story of redemption—the act of being saved. As I share my testimony, you'll hear about my transformative journey from merely knowing Jesus to experiencing the profound reality of being truly known by Him. I've moved from a place of only encountering Jesus on Sundays to a deeper, more intimate relationship, where trust and faith guide me daily. He has become the one I turn to for guidance in my decisions and the source of comfort when I am unsure if I have the strength to continue. In my journey, I have learned to let go of the things that once defined my identity and focus on how I can be more Christlike in everything I do. This transformation hasn't been easy, but it has been the most freeing and restorative experience of my life.

> "You will seek me and find me when you seek me with all your heart" (Jeremiah 29:13, NIV).

JESUS ENCOUNTER: THE DEFINING MOMENT

I've lived much of my life in a state of half-truth. I grew up in church, knew Jesus, and studied the Bible. I was baptized at twelve and went on several international mission trips to share Christ's love with children who might never have heard about Him. I listened to Christian music to center my day and attended church regularly. But as I entered adulthood—what I call "adulting"—life took hold in ways I hadn't anticipated. Bad moments happened, and unexplained pain cast its shadow, bringing destruction to my family and often allowing circumstances to define who I was.

I experienced anger and bitterness toward those who hurt me, clinging tightly to the illusion of controlling every aspect of my life. If I am honest, this half-truth way of living leaves little room for God to work through us and advance His kingdom. By remaining in a negative or busy mindset, we limit the beautiful and amazing gifts God has for us because we fail to see them. Instead of being intentional and embracing abundance and worthiness, I became reactive, focusing on what could go wrong rather than on the abundance God offers.

> *By remaining in a negative or busy mindset, we limit the beautiful and amazing gifts God has for us because we fail to see them.*

My healing journey—both inside and out—began in 2023. I was deeply frustrated with my weight and how I felt and looked. My self-esteem was at an all-time low, and I harbored a negative view of my appearance. Others, however, did not see me that way. From the outside, I appeared fulfilled, doing all the right things to portray an image of stability, happiness, and success. Yet, internally, I was breaking down.

People saw a cheerful, engaging person who smiled at everyone she met, but the truth was my emotions were scattered. I struggled to focus, and I faced persistent inflammation, migraines, and joint pain. The tasks that consumed my time left me feeling overwhelmed, making the ideas of eating right and exercising seem impossible. The effort to maintain an outward appearance of well-being was masking the turmoil I felt inside. One day, I prayed, "Please, Jesus, help me in this area of my life. I know I have not given my health to you or asked for guidance, but I give it to you now."

Jesus has faithfully walked with me through some of the darkest times in my life, yet I realized I had never fully surrendered my health to Him. I clung to a victim mentality and allowed stress to consume me to the point where I was harming myself with the negative thoughts I held onto. This mindset even affected my relationships, distancing me from those around me. I couldn't accept a compliment; if someone, even my husband, said, "You look pretty," or "I like your outfit," I would immediately dismiss it. I made countless excuses for not addressing my health—blaming my demanding professional career, our small family business, and the time spent caring for the kids. I convinced myself I simply didn't have time to do the necessary work, inside and out, to address the root issues and the emotional pain I was still carrying.

I prayed for guidance, asking God to connect me with people who could help me in this area of my life. I sought His help to give me the motivation, wisdom, and confidence to lose a few pounds, knowing I wanted to do it naturally to reduce inflammation, regain my ability to move, and restore my energy. At that time, I was forty-nine—what some might call a midlife crisis. But it wasn't just an emotional struggle; physically, I was operating at about 15 percent of my total capacity. My days consisted of eating, working nine-to-five, and then sleeping. That was it. I had no energy for anything else because of how terrible I felt, and I was relying heavily on over-the-counter pain medication just to get by. I finally reached a point when I knew something had to change—enough was enough.

I truly believe that after we come to God in prayer, He calls us to take action. We need to do our part and not just passively wait for something to fall into our laps. After praying for help in this area of my life, God moved swiftly. A friend at work told me about a holistic wellness center that had helped her, and she suggested I check it out. I took

> *I truly believe that after we come to God in prayer, He calls us to take action.*

that as a nudge from God and made an appointment the very next day. At the center, I had a full panel of blood work done to assess my hormone and glucose levels. This marked the beginning of my journey to take responsibility for my health.

It turned out there was a reason for my inability to cope with the world around me—my hormones were imbalanced. For so long, I thought my irritability, confusion, dizziness, headaches, fatigue, and difficulty concentrating were just part of life, something I had to endure. But when the doctor came in with my lab results, I finally had an answer. My blood sugar was low, my iron levels were low, and I was diagnosed with diabetes. On top of that, my cholesterol wasn't just high—it was off-the-charts "bad." At that moment, everything began to make sense. What I had been experiencing wasn't just stress or overwhelm; my body had been signaling for help, and I needed to listen.

I had been holding on to the idea that to be loved and fully live in God's love, I had to prove my value and worth as the world defined them. What changed for me was my decision to release these areas fully while praying and walking daily with Christ. Up to that point, I had lived for everyone else. Like most moms, I put my children's needs and wants above my own—after all, isn't that what we are called to do as mothers? But as I sat in the doctor's office, absorbing the news about my health, I had a stark realization: I had not been showing up for myself. If something didn't change—if I didn't start taking care of my body through better eating habits, exercise, and time with God—I wouldn't be there for my family much longer. It was a sobering thought that shifted my perspective. Taking care of myself wasn't just for me; it was for them too.

I realized if I wanted to truly heal and get better, my priorities needed to shift. For nearly three decades, I had built a successful career that I loved, traveled internationally, connected with executives, and coached Technology professionals on leadership development and how to have joy in the workplace. In addition to my professional life, I

> *I realized if I wanted to truly heal and get better, my priorities needed to shift.*

was a dedicated wife and parent to my two adult sons and our youngest, who was in middle school. My husband and I were also co-owners of a lavender farm and online business called Sweet Streams Lavender.

While these roles were fulfilling, they consumed so much of my energy that I began to see the toll they were taking on my own well-being. It was time to place my health first not only for my own sake but for the well-being of my family and the people I cared about.

I joined a community of fellow believers to begin the inner work needed to center myself toward Christ. I recognized there were areas in my life where I needed to take responsibility to truly get better. With the support of my personal life coach, weekly community meetings, and guidance from speakers and wellness coaches, I started making meaningful changes. I continued seeing my wellness doctor monthly and committed to my physical and spiritual growth.

I have always thrived on meeting new people and seeking opportunities to grow. However, as I began to focus more on my health, I realized that maintaining this high level of energy and control was becoming unsustainable. It was clear to me that God was calling me to something more significant—leading others to Christ. This realization was a turning point, redirecting my focus from simply managing my life to fulfilling a greater purpose and calling.

It took a year of surrendering these areas of my life to God and committing to internal and external work to achieve significant health improvements. I worked diligently to reduce my weight, lower inflammation, eliminate diabetes, and balance my hormones. However, at the end of 2023, I ended up in the hospital for five days. This was a pivotal moment that revealed I still had not fully surrendered. It became clear that God was asking me to completely trust Him with my health and slow down in order to really hear Him. In the silence, I could clearly see the new direction for my life as an author. I felt God calling me to use my voice through writing and guest appearances on podcasts to share the challenging and dark areas of my life, offering encouragement and hope to others through my journey of healing and obedience.

SONG OF TRUTH

At the beginning of 2024, I underwent a total hysterectomy as a result of being hospitalized for ovarian cysts that had ruptured. During this time of healing, God led me to co-author a book called The Joy-Full Entrepreneur: Awaken, Renew, Transform, an Amazon best-seller, which was released in November 2024. I share my story of letting go of the need for control and trusting my life fully to God. It was through this period of surrender and asking for Jesus's help that I experienced a profound transformation. Instead of just losing a few pounds, I lost fifty pounds over the course of the year. I had to make significant changes to my diet, including reducing sugars, regulating my hormones, and monitoring portion sizes. This required a lot of discipline and restraint, and it was only by returning to God that I was able to achieve this. Without His guidance, I knew I would likely revert to old habits.

After a year, I started exercising and discovered a joy I had never experienced before. I began taking mile-long walks during work breaks. This allowed me to return to my tasks with increased productivity, far surpassing what I could accomplish by sitting at my desk for hours.

My oldest son recently returned home to Kansas for a few weeks. He encouraged me to go to the gym with him. He said he would help motivate and coach me so that when he returned home to Connecticut, I would have a solid routine to follow. From that experience, I felt so much love from my son and knew he truly cared about my well-being. It then became a challenge for me, and if you know me, I have a bit of a competitive spirit.

Throughout this journey, I struggled and felt like giving up, always doubting my own strength. Yet, God faithfully brought people into my life who offered support and encouragement. I joined a community of Christian entrepreneurs who meet weekly. This group has provided a safe place for me to share the significant impact these changes were having on my business and family.

This journey was far from easy, but I believe Christ served as my guide during this time, demonstrating the character qualities of grace, gentleness, faithfulness, and self-control.

"You Say," by Lauren Daigle, is a song of truth, reminding us that God says we are loved, even when we do not feel it. We can continue to trust in his love for us. We are not who the world says we are.

BECOMING MORE LIKE CHRIST

Addressing the heart work was crucial for me. I realized I had accumulated a great deal of bitterness that was preventing me from living a life that mirrored Christ. My tendency to control every aspect of my life, including my family and work, was rooted in this bitterness and pride. Healing from it and aligning my life with Christ required faith, surrender, and intentional practice.

Faithfulness is a defining character quality of Christ that I lean into. In moments of pruning, growth, and learning to be obedient, I hold fast to Christ's faithfulness—a steadfast commitment to God's plan, even in the face of suffering (Hebrews 3:2).

Here are some steps that helped me in this process:

1. **Acknowledge the Bitterness:** Recognize and admit that bitterness exists in your heart. Often, it arises from unresolved hurt, disappointment, or unforgiveness. Acknowledging its presence is the first step toward healing.

    Isaiah 41:10 guides you through unresolved hurt and disappointment, reminding you God is with you, and He will strengthen and help you.

2. **Seek God in Prayer:** Spend time in prayer, asking God to reveal the areas where bitterness is rooted in your heart. Pray for a softened heart and the strength to forgive, let go, and heal.

    Psalm 139:23-24 is a powerful prayer that asks God to search your heart and reveal any harmful ways within you.

3. **Forgive Others:** Forgiveness is essential for healing. It doesn't mean condoning what happened; instead, it involves releasing the hold it has on your heart.

    Ephesians 4:31-32 instructs you to put away bitterness and forgive others as Christ forgave you.

4. **Surrender Control:** Bitterness often stems from unmet expectations or a need to control outcomes. Surrender your control to God, trusting He has a plan and purpose for your life, even when things haven't gone as *you* planned.

    Proverbs 3:5-6 reminds you to trust in the Lord with all your heart and not rely on your own understanding.

For the past year, I've been on a transformative journey of refinement, learning to live a life that truly reflects the love of Christ. Though I have always known Jesus, my relationship with Him had not yet deepened beyond familiarity. Now I walk with Him daily. It is a faith-filled journey where His presence surrounds me—guiding, comforting, and strengthening me each step of the way through His Word and prayer. I encourage you to ask God to reveal the areas in your life where you are truly seen and heard, places where His stability and presence are already at work.

God winks are unexpected moments when God reveals a tangible sign of what He's doing in your life. It is that moment when your heart realizes God is present. I think it is His way of getting our attention. I pray that after reading this, God will give you a wink … a reminder of how much He cares for you.

> *God winks are unexpected moments when God reveals a tangible sign of what He's doing in your life.*

Heavenly Father, thank you for your unfailing love. Thank you for allowing us to come to you with all our requests and that you see and hear us. Thank you for pursuing us, even when we can't see you. Thank you for your Word that teaches us how to believe, trust, and share your love with others. We live in your truth and desire a deeper relationship with you, Jesus. Amen.

How might your life be transformed if you fully trusted God's love and His calling for you, letting go of the fears and barriers that keep you from truly experiencing the abundant life?

pray

Reflect

Write

CHRISTINA, A.K.A. "CHRISSY," BLINCOE is a child of God, chosen by Him and held up by His grace and love for fifty years. She is a wife to her sweet hubby Joe and a momma to three amazing sons: Brandon, Trenton, and Isaac. Joe and Chrissy are both active in their church family, where they have dedicated over twenty-four years to serving in various leadership roles. She gives back her time and heart to others and has a deep desire and drive to leave a legacy for her children.

Chrissy presently works for an employee-owned engineering firm. Throughout her twenty-eight-year career, she has worked with similar firms, learning what being an entrepreneur means and the mindset and spirit behind it. She has a heart to serve with her gifts in technology and business. Chrissy is a business owner, engineer, speaker, author, mentor, coach, and connector.

She volunteers with young people and women entrepreneurs to share her experience in small business. Along with her Master's Degree in Business Relationship Management, she and her husband are the *joy-full entrepreneurs* behind Sweet Streams Lavender.

Joe and Chrissy started their lavender farm in Kansas ten years ago, focusing on each other's strengths to utilize their time effectively and create intentional connections with their community. The mission of Sweet Streams Lavender is grounded in faith, values, and love for family, friends, partners, and customers they call "friends." Joe and Chrissy are here to help others find the beauty in themselves, and God is not done with them yet. Check out her contribution to the cohort book, *The Joy-Full Entrepreneur: Awaken, Renew, Transform,* released in November 2024.

Sanctification is the lifelong process of becoming less like ourselves and more like Jesus.

Heather Demorest

Chapter 12

Going through the Motions
By Heather Demorest

Sanctification is the lifelong process of becoming less like ourselves and more like Jesus.

Becoming more like Jesus . . . oh, if it were only as easy as rising out of the water after we proclaim He is the Christ, son of the living God. Instead, it's a lifelong journey full of twists, turns, storms, pain, and learning to die to self each day. It's also a journey of joy, peace, trust, obedience, growth, and faith—a journey where all of these pieces are played out in a perfectly timed waltz, orchestrated by God.

> *Becoming more like Jesus . . . oh, if it were only as easy as rising out of the water after we proclaim He is the Christ, son of the living God.*

The sun was shining brightly through the windshield of my Ford Expedition. I was alone. My husband and kids had left nearly two hours before me. My heart and my mind were conflicted with each other. My mind felt chaotic. My heart was . . . well, numb. I wanted to be at home on my couch. There was a marathon of my favorite true-crime television show running, and my pajamas were bunched in a ball on the floor of my room. My favorite blanket was folded up on the couch, and my half-empty cup of coffee was left abandoned on the counter. Instead of being home in my safe space, cuddled up on my couch, I was in the car driving north to a place I wasn't sure I wanted to be—and wearing *real* pants!

My mind was processing why I was resistant to going to church. It had been weeks since I attended. I loved Jesus. He loved me. My kids were at church. My husband was on the children's ministry team. Why didn't I want to go? Was I angry? Was I sad? Was it real? Was it a waste of time? Something was seriously off. Life was hard, and I was miserable. I didn't like my job, my husband, my kids, my family, or myself. I had isolated myself and put nearly everyone at a distance. Sundays had become the day my family went to church and I stayed home—on the couch, in my pajamas, watching true-crime TV or an MTV reality show.

As I rounded the on-ramp to the interstate, heading north to the church, WayFM played softly in the background. The song "The Motions," by Matthew West, began. As I listened, my heart was pierced in the deepest part of my soul. How did I get here? How did I get to this point? At seventeen, I was so excited to find Jesus. He had been pursuing me relentlessly my entire life. He had protected me, provided for me, and walked beside me. He had called out to me—all of this when I didn't really know Him. I knew *of* Him, but I did not *know* Him on a personal level—His character, His heart, His mission, His love for me. He had always been there. So what was missing? I was baptized. We had the kids dedicated. We took them to church, sent them to camp, and involved them in church activities. I spent many a Sunday in the pews, listening to the sermons and singing the worship songs. How was it that I was now a thirty-something married mom of six who was indifferent and resistant to showing up for worship and the message? I shouldn't feel like this, right? Matthew West summed it up through his lyrics. That was me. I had been going through the motions.

The years of attending church added up to nothing more than checked boxes on my "Christian Girl Bingo card." For years, I had been showing up, singing the songs, hearing the words, and resuming *my* life for the next six days . . . lather, rinse, repeat. This had been my life for way too long following that

> *My heart, not unlike my favorite TV show, was a crime scene! The little chalk outline of this crime scene was a perfectly shaped, Jesus-sized hole inside my heart—a hole longing to be filled.*

salvation moment in the tiny house converted to a church on Murfreesboro Road. I was saved, but I still didn't *know* Jesus! Suddenly, I was broken. As my heart began to feel at that moment, I was exhausted, upset, and lost. My heart, not unlike my favorite TV show, was a crime scene! The little chalk outline of this crime scene was a perfectly shaped, Jesus-sized hole inside my heart—a hole longing to be filled. Tears flowed down my cheeks. What was happening?

When I joined my family at church that Sunday morning, God continued to speak into my soul. It was profound. Our worship leader stood on stage and sang "Broken," by Lifehouse. My emotions overcame me. Tears welled up in my eyes and ran down my cheeks. Once again, I knew this was me. I was the person singing the song—me. I was falling apart. I was barely breathing. My broken heart was barely beating. At that moment, my thirty-some years of life caught up with me—the abandonment, the rejection, the sadness, the mistakes, the lost opportunities, the faults, and the fears. The things I had hidden and stuffed into the deepest crevices of my heart and soul suddenly came to the surface. As the tears continued to roll, I felt a release. Is this what had been filling the Jesus-shaped hole in my heart? Somehow, I needed to let it go and clear the junk filling the void where Jesus should be. I needed Jesus desperately. I prayed. I felt. And that was the day I began to heal.

> "Suppose one of you has a hundred sheep and loses one of them. Doesn't he leave the ninety-nine in the open country and go after the lost sheep until he finds it? And when he finds it, he joyfully puts it on his shoulders and goes home. Then he calls his friends and neighbors together and says, 'Rejoice with me; I have found my lost sheep.' I tell you that in the same way there will be more rejoicing in heaven over one sinner who repents than over ninety-nine righteous persons who do not need to repent"
> (Luke 15:4–7, NIV).

I love the parable of the lost sheep. It's a beautiful picture of the importance of the *one*! In this world, we can often feel alone, unwanted, unseen, or worthless. This was me . . . the girl who realized she was broken and just going through the motions. This passage shows how incredibly valuable we are to Jesus. He may have ninety-nine others, but He wants us! He chooses us! He sees us! He notices our absence! He will chase us down each time we stray and joyfully bring us back to himself.

We took a family trip to Disney when our children were small. My youngest daughter turned four a couple of months before. We were about to get in line for a ride, but I had to park the stroller. While the rest of the family made their way to the line, she stayed with me, holding onto my belt loop. That was always the rule. If I can't hold on to your hand, hold on to my belt loop. I parked the stroller, grabbed the bag, and proceeded across the walkway to meet the rest of the family. When I approached my husband, he asked, "Where is Stephanie?" I turned in horror to find she was no longer holding onto my belt loop. I ran from the line into the crowd, looking for her. My heart and soul felt as if they left my body. My precious baby girl was gone, and I needed to find her.

I stood on the large walkway, yelling for her and scanning each child and family! Tears were welling up when, suddenly, I saw her standing in the walkway, alone and crying. I ran to her, picked her up, and hugged her tightly. She said to me, "There was a butterfly."

"It's okay, sweetie," I said as I ran back to our family, announcing that she was found. We all celebrated. In my mind, I like to believe that when one believer wanders off, this is how Jesus feels. We are cherished. He will search for us. He will scoop us up and celebrate, but we must be willing to be found.

> *He will search for us. He will scoop us up and celebrate, but we must be willing to be found.*

In *my* moment of being lost, He knew I wasn't strong on my own. In His grace, He brought me a friend named Miranda. To know her is to be near to Jesus. She's kind, loving, and has a heart to serve others. We met through church. She was my daughter's camp counselor. I didn't know her at the time. I couldn't remember her name, but my husband thought she was fabulous.

She gave us a freezer she was getting rid of, as we needed one for our brood! I remember him telling me about her, and she and I became friends on Facebook.

My husband and I were walking through a difficult season of life. Chaos seemed to surround us. One night, Miranda posted on Facebook that they needed assistance for VBS, as one of the skit team members was injured and could not participate. I commented something funny and cute, but she reached out. She asked if I was seriously interested. I had nothing better to do and needed a distraction from life, so I said sure! We went from being "Facebook friends" to being real friends in what felt like an instant. She was so kind to my family and me. She saw the things we were walking through, stood with me, and loved and prayed us through them. Through her, I began to see a light—a passion. I began to see Jesus in human form—not that she was Jesus, but she was how we are to model His life, how we are to model His service. Through helping her with VBS, I was ministered to! I was learning alongside the kiddos we were teaching. I was learning how to be a follower of Christ! She'll never realize how that one post on Facebook changed my life or how getting to know her helped save me. She loved me in my brokenness. She never made me feel judged. She would pray with me and lead me through the Scriptures when I needed prayer.

My family and I joined the small group led by Miranda and her husband. We began doing life together, along with several other families. Suddenly, I was surrounded by Christian friends who prayed with and over our family.

> ... a relationship with God and Jesus is not about what I've done or haven't done. It's about what Jesus has done!

I was in the Word. I was leaning into God and His character. I was learning how to have a relationship with Jesus. I watched Miranda love and serve others in a manner counterintuitive to culture. Her friendship strengthened me at a time when I was weak. Her Faith strengthened me at a time when I was floundering. Her love covered my brokenness when I was at my lowest. Through her, I learned that a relationship with God and Jesus is not about what I've done or haven't done. It's about what Jesus has done! It's about God's unfailing love. Jesus wasn't physically here to chase me down and carry me back, but He sent a friend who did just that. He continued to bless me over the next few years with several more faithful Christian friends who had vastly different walks with the Lord. They were all different in personality and gifts. They were each such a blessing and played an integral role in my growth. I learned from each of them by watching their actions, their faithfulness, and their obedience to the Lord.

I met my friend Jessica in 2018 through business. She and I became fast friends. We had much in common and shared many similar life experiences. This woman taught me about prayer and faithfully waiting on God. She taught me about the value of relationships, even from afar, as she lives 1,200 miles from me. Her love and prayers were powerful, and she taught me about the goodness of a gentle heart. My sweet friend Angela, whom I met at a conference, has also inspired me. She has walked me closer to Jesus many times through the Scriptures, Bible study, and prayer. She is a testament to God's faithfulness and how to walk boldly and courageously. I have observed her as a servant leader in her company and community and have watched her remain faithful during some challenging times. I have been blessed to have many other mentors and friends in my life. I wouldn't be who I am today without them—or Jesus.

At seventeen, I thought being baptized was it! That's how you have a good life. Find Jesus. Decide to give Him your life. Climb in the water and come out as His—signed, sealed, and delivered! But it's not that simple. It's an everyday practice to grow in God, to grow closer to Him, and to become who He created you to be. There is joy in the journey, but you have to be an active participant. There are days I still feel like a baby Christian. I don't know all the Scriptures. My recall of exact verses is not always on par, but He doesn't mind. I'm a continual work in progress.

The day I married my husband, I knew him. I loved him. It's taken twenty-seven years to know him as I do today. It has required daily intention, choosing and serving him, walking in humility, and seeing him the way Jesus sees him.

We invest in our relationship. How? We talk. We spend time together. Every relationship requires effort on both parts. Jesus has done His part. He wants us to do ours. He wants us to sit with Him each day, to talk to Him about our hopes and fears, and to bring our struggles and burdens to Him. He seeks us each day. Do we seek Him? Whether you are a new Christian or a lifelong follower of Jesus, how is your relationship? Do you put Him first? Are you talking to Him daily? Are you spending time in the Word daily? All of these are vital for a healthy relationship with Him.

The peace, contentment, and joy that bloom from a relationship with God cannot be obtained through any other means. That Jesus-shaped hole in my heart is now healed. He is the filter across that gap. I'm not defined by my years of feeling abandoned. I'm not defined by past mistakes. I'm not defined by any mistakes I make now. I'm not what the world tells me to be. I'm a chosen, worthy, protected daughter of the King. God is working on my heart daily. Sometimes, I still feel like a mess. He still has a lot of pruning to do. The difference is I am not soothing my inner mess by hiding from Him. I'm no longer going through the motions. I now have an all-consuming passion for the Lord inside me. I crave His Word and learning about who He is. Yes, I still make mistakes. Yes, I have a long way to go on my journey. He'll be pruning, refining, and transforming me until I meet Him face-to-face. Sweet friends, be encouraged. If God left the ninety-nine for me, you can be sure He's coming to find you too!

Christ is faithful.

> "Jesus Christ is the same yesterday and today and forever" (Hebrews 13:8, NIV).

> "But the Lord is faithful, and he will strengthen you and protect you from the evil one" (2 Thessalonians 3:3, NIV).

> "Because of the LORD's great love we are not consumed, for his compassions never fail. They are new every morning; great is your faithfulness" (Lamentations 3:22–23, NIV).

Where are you in your faith journey (new follower, longtime follower, not quite there), and what is one step you can take today to step closer to Jesus?

pray

Reflect

Write

HEATHER DEMOREST is a three-time best-selling author, gratitude journal creator, and Christian motivational speaker who dedicates her life to helping others embrace the love of Jesus and live out their unique purpose. As the founder of Aligned by Faith, she encourages others to align their lives with spiritual principles and personal growth. A registered nurse, wife, mother of six, and former clinical team manager, Heather combines her professional expertise with a passion for ministry, inspiring others to thrive in faith and purpose.

Sanctification is like God giving me a new gift each day, inviting me to open it, use it, and be in awe of His provision while wrestling with my pride, wanting to do it myself, and seeking praise. It's a daily process of learning to surrender and trusting that His gift is what truly transforms me, even when I resist like a child.

Kess Scharff

Chapter 13

Embracing the Unknown
By Kess Scharff

Sanctification is like God giving me a new gift each day, inviting me to open it, use it, and be in awe of His provision while wrestling with my pride, wanting to do it myself, and seeking praise. It's a daily process of learning to surrender and trusting that His gift is what truly transforms me, even when I resist like a child.

This life is full of hills and valleys. By letting go of my need for comfort and control, I learned to let the Holy Spirit work through me so people could see Jesus's love. This was a hard choice—owning my mistakes, sacrificing my comfort, and walking out in faith. It involved truly trusting that God is good and understanding that through *sanctification,* this life is just a brief moment in the face of eternity.

THE MOMENT OF DESPAIR

I sat in a cold metal chair, surrounded by others, wondering how I ended up here and desperately wishing to wake up from this nightmare. My family didn't know how to handle what I was going through. They were hurt, confused, sad, and disappointed. It felt like they despised me, but in reality, they just didn't know how to process their emotions or trust me, and why should they? I couldn't escape the thought that I deserved to be here. My mind felt trapped, and my body was utterly exhausted. I felt like discarded gum—stuck to the road and run over again and again. Shame overwhelmed me, and guilt consumed my thoughts. How did I lose everything? I felt unworthy of love, invisible to the world. Even the simplest movements felt impossible. Each day felt like an insurmountable mountain, and I wondered if I deserved to get up.

It seemed easier to remain trapped in this cycle of regret and shame, unable to see a way out. The dream of nurturing my family and providing them with the love I so desperately longed for had crumbled. I had tried so hard to protect them from the pain I experienced growing up, but in doing so, I lost control of my life and inflicted a deep wound on my family. Have you ever felt that way—like you're carrying the weight of the world, responsible for everyone's happiness, only to watch everything fall apart? That's where I found myself. I was stuck in a cycle of regret, wondering if I'd ever be able to breathe again.

THE LIE OF CONTROL

I thought that by controlling every situation, person, and outcome, I could protect my loved ones from pain. But that was the lie. I had taken on the burden of fixing everything—an impossible task. It was a cycle of regret, born of trauma, where choice seemed like an illusion. Trauma survivors often cling to control as a way to avoid pain. Sitting in that cold chair, I was reminded that I had another choice. God spoke to my heart: "You can stay in this cycle, or you can trust me and heal." His promise was not that life would be easy but that in trusting Him, transformation could happen.

Maybe you've felt trapped, too, believing there's no way out of your pain. But God offers us another option. He asks us to trust Him, let go of control, and allow Him to heal our hearts.

God's voice pierced through my darkest moment, and that revelation lifted a weight off my chest.

THE CHOICE TO TRUST

Trusting God, especially after experiencing deep hurt, can feel impossible. How do you trust when the people who should have protected you caused the most harm? How do you trust when life has only given you pain? God didn't ask me to trust blindly; He asked me to see my situation through His eyes. He knew my pain and was asking me to release it to Him.

> *How do you trust when life has only given you pain?*

Galatians 6:9 (NIV) became my lifeline: "Let us not become weary in doing good, for at the proper time we will reap a harvest if we do not give up." Trust wasn't about having all the answers. It was about surrendering control and choosing to believe that God's plan was better than mine.

LOT'S WIFE

In Genesis 19, we read of Lot's wife who looked back at the city of Sodom as it was being destroyed by God, even though she was told not to. She clung to the familiarity of her past, and it cost her her life, turning her into a pillar of salt. I didn't want to be like her—stuck in my pain, unwilling to move forward toward a new life.

How many of us stay stuck, clinging to the past because it feels familiar, even though we know it might be holding us back from something better? Maybe you feel the same way, trapped in what's comfortable, even though it's hurting you. I was like her—afraid to move forward, clinging to the familiar. But God is offering something new: a future where we don't have to carry the burdens of yesterday. Trust Him with the unknown.

GOD'S LOVE FOR ME

It's easy to understand God's love in theory, but believing it in your heart is different. I struggled with feeling unworthy of love. Childhood abuse had left me feeling broken, and I made choices that only deepened my shame.

For years, I believed I was unworthy of love. I thought I deserved the pain. Maybe you feel that way, too, like you don't deserve anything good because of what you've been through or the choices you've made. Perhaps you've felt like you're not worthy of love or redemption. The world teaches us that love is something we earn, but God's love isn't like that. He loves you simply because He created you.

> "For you created my inmost being; you knit me together in my mother's womb. I praise you because I am fearfully and wonderfully made; your works are wonderful, I know that full well" (Psalm 139:13–14, NIV).

I had to learn that my worth wasn't based on what I could achieve or how perfect I could be. God was collecting every tear I cried, and each one mattered to Him and is recorded (Psalm 56:8). You are not alone in your pain. God sees you. He knows the struggles you've faced, and He loves you deeply, just as you are.

THE DAY I BROKE

In my darkest moment, I swallowed a bottle of pills, desperate to end the unbearable pain of deep depression, hopelessness, and endless anguish. In that instant, I felt numb and disconnected from everything, including the consequences of my actions. Perhaps you've experienced a similar feeling—like you're drowning, with no hope of coming up for air.

But even in that moment, God didn't abandon me. I didn't realize it then, but He was with me, and through the Holy Spirit, He was working in the hearts of those around me. I felt utterly broken, yet even in that place, God was moving.

I found myself hospitalized, feeling like a prisoner in my own body and stripped of dignity and hope. But it was there, in my lowest moment, that God showed me His love. The Holy Spirit moved through my husband who offered love and compassion even when he had every right to be angry. Slowly, I began to understand that no mistake is too big for God to redeem.

He didn't want me to stay stuck in shame. He wanted me to trust Him and believe He could redeem even my darkest day. His love hadn't abandoned me, even when I thought all hope was lost. Gradually, He revealed His plan for redemption.

> "And we know that in all things God works for the good of those who love him, who have been called according to his purpose" (Romans 8:28, NIV).

REDEMPTION AND A NEW LEGACY

In that sterile, cold place, I saw glimpses of hope. I learned God doesn't waste our pain. Every tear, every moment of despair, is used for good when we give it to Him. My story of brokenness became a testimony of His grace. The journey of healing wasn't instant, but God was faithful. My lowest point became the starting place for a new journey. He turned my greatest failure into the foundation of my redemption. What felt like the end was actually the beginning of a new life that I never imagined could come from such pain.

Through the Holy Spirit, I began a journey of healing. He took the broken pieces of my life and pieced them back together. He turned my despair into a story of hope. Maybe you're in a similar place—feeling like your story is over. But God sees you. He knows your pain and wants to redeem even the darkest parts of your life. You don't have to go through it alone.

God gave me a new perspective on my pain by using it to strengthen my faith and help others. I could see the value in my suffering, knowing it wasn't wasted. God had trusted me enough to steward this pain well and let it be used for His glory. My story is becoming one of continuous redemption, a testimony of God's continued faithfulness.

Today, I share my story not as someone who has it all together but as someone who has experienced God's redeeming love. I speak nationally and internationally, guiding those in their wrestling, helping them identify areas that can be challenged, reminding them that the Holy Spirit is with them, and encouraging them to choose faith over fear and healing over shame. The journey isn't over, but I trust God with every step. His love is the foundation on which I build, knowing He is good and redeems all things. He's there, offering healing and hope, changing the course of generational sin—if we choose to trust Him. God doesn't waste our pain.

I'll never forget the day I sat in that metal chair and made the hardest decision of my life—to surrender my way for God's way. That choice changed everything not just for me but for my family and generations to come. At that moment, I handed over my relationships, my guilt, and my fear of failure as a parent to the Lord. It wasn't easy to stick to the hard path He called me to, especially when I felt overwhelmed with blame for the struggles my children were walking through. I often wanted to avoid being the "parent" and let grace outweigh boundaries, but God showed me a better way.

Through the tumultuous teen years, God guided me, teaching me to parent with intentionality instead of guilt. He reminded me that love doesn't excuse poor behavior or give a free pass to avoid hard lessons it holds firm in truth and grace. I could have let my shame paralyze me, leading to a legacy of brokenness. But by His mercy, I didn't. Instead, I chose to obey God, even when it was difficult. I set boundaries, leaned into His wisdom, and trusted Him to fill in the gaps where I fell short.

> *Love doesn't excuse poor behavior or give a free pass to avoid hard lessons*

Today, I stand in awe of the fruits of that decision. My three daughters have grown into incredible women who love Jesus with all their hearts. They don't take the easy way out but walk in wisdom and integrity. As I watch them build loving marriages and model godly values for their own children, I see the ripple effect of redemption. The legacy of broken patterns and generational sin stops here because God transformed my heart and guided our family through the hard work of change.

This journey has taught me the decisions we make today—however painful or inconvenient—carry eternal weight. God's faithfulness extends beyond what we can see, even when the world tells us we're doing it wrong. His plan is always worth following. now see how He was weaving His goodness into our story, even when I didn't understand. Because we chose to surrender and let Him lead, my grandchildren will inherit a new legacy.

> *This journey has taught me that the decisions we make today—however painful or inconvenient—carry eternal weight.*

THE POWER OF CHOICE

Every day, God gives you a choice. You can continue to carry the burdens of shame and regret, or you can choose to trust God with your pain. It may not seem easy, but God doesn't expect you to take huge leaps all at once. It may not seem like much, but even the smallest step can lead to healing. Sometimes, it's about taking small, simple steps—and that's enough. Maybe today, that step is simply recognizing when you're speaking negatively to yourself. Noticing the lies you've believed is the first step toward healing. Take a moment to notice when those thoughts creep in. If you catch yourself thinking, *I'm not enough,* or *I'll never change,* stop. Call that moment a victory—because it is. You're beginning to recognize the lies that hold you back, and that's a powerful step toward healing. This became my everyday practice, and it was exhausting but so rewarding, as I know change happens from one moment to the next.

Every time you catch yourself thinking negatively, replace it with truth: *God loves me; I am worthy; I am seen.* You don't have to feel it yet—that will come in time—but simply saying it is an act of faith. Each small choice you make to notice, to shift your thinking, and to believe the truth is a win. Celebrate each step, no matter how small it seems. God celebrates with you, and each step brings you closer to the peace and freedom He has for you. Remember, progress is progress, no matter how small it may seem.

So, what is your one step today? Can you catch just one negative thought? Can you replace it with a truth about who you are in Christ? That's all you need to do for now. One step. One victory. One moment of progress.

Let today be the day you recognize and celebrate the small victories in your life. Trust that God is at work within you, faithfully completing the good work He has begun. You are seen. You are heard. You are loved. This is more than just a feeling; it's faith in action.

Today, choose your perspective. If I could, I would love to grab a coffee or take a walk with you—those are my favorite ways to talk about life. Please know that I'm cheering for you and praying over you because it's no accident that you're reading this. You have a powerful, redeeming story within you! Remember, you can do hard things! I would love to hear your story.

LOVING THROUGH THE PAIN: HOPE AND STRENGTH FOR THOSE WHO SUPPORT THE STRUGGLING

I could not close my chapter without addressing all of those who suffer and those who love them. It's hard to imagine the depth of pain felt by those who watch a loved one living in agony and feel powerless to help. The confusion and heartache over why someone would want to leave this world can be overwhelming. It's important to understand that in those moments of deep despair, people aren't thinking about others—they're consumed by a mental anguish that blocks out everything else. We live in a world that encourages us to act on our feelings, often without realizing that these feelings, even the darkest ones, can pass.

So many people aren't equipped with the tools, self-care practices, or compassionate support that would help them realize they don't have to be stuck in this cycle. They may not have been shown the hope found within Scripture or how to extend grace to themselves. For those who love someone struggling with suicidal thoughts, it's incredibly painful. They see the value in their loved one, a value that person can't see in themselves. They may not understand that their loved one feels as if they're walking around in a "body cast" of emotional pain. And asking them to "just get better" feels as impossible as asking someone with broken bones to get up and run.

There's often a lack of understanding about what mental anguish looks like, and even those who try to help may find themselves exhausted and frustrated. In their love and pain, they might struggle to understand and wonder if they're losing themselves, too, as they try to make things better, not realizing this approach can sometimes create distance instead of comfort.

My husband showed up for me in the hardest moments in ways I can only attribute to God's strength working in him. He could have been angry, sad, or confused—and he was, at times. But he chose to stand by me, keeping his vow of "in sickness and in health." Sometimes, we forget that marriage often calls us to be holy more than happy. Happiness can be fleeting, but the holiness of love is a steady, enduring joy that can carry us through even the hardest trials. He was a warrior for our family, helping our daughters to process their pain and confusion while also making space for me to heal.

There is hope, even in the darkest seasons. If you're struggling, know these feelings can pass and healing is possible. Please don't hesitate to reach out to mental health professionals who are trained to help you navigate this journey. Counselors, therapists, and other specialized professionals can provide the support, guidance, and tools to help you move forward. You don't have to do this alone. And if you're supporting someone, remember that being present with love and compassion is powerful, but helping your loved one connect with the right professionals can be life-changing. Healing is possible, and there are tools, faith, and people who can help guide you along the way.

There's a way through, and hope is within reach.

"May the God of hope fill you with all joy and peace as you trust in him, so that you may overflow with hope by the power of the Holy Spirit" (Romans 15:13, NIV).

Christ is trustworthy.

> "Jesus Christ is the same yesterday, today, and forever" (Hebrews 13:8, NLT).

> "For your kingdom is an everlasting kingdom. You rule throughout all generations. The LORD always keeps his promises; he is gracious in all he does" (Psalm 145:13, NLT).

Each time you catch a negative thought and choose to replace it with truth, you're claiming a victory—a small, beautiful step forward.

Can you take a moment right now to name one negative thought and gently exchange it for a truth about who God says you are?

That's it. Just one thought. One truth. One step toward freedom. Celebrate this moment of progress—you're moving forward, and that matters.

pray

Reflect

KESS SCHARFF is the founder and CEO of SEEDS for Change, an organization dedicated to empowering individuals to become the best versions of themselves by fostering physical and emotional wellness. Her innovative approach encourages people to overcome pain through playful and creative challenges, helping individuals from diverse backgrounds achieve transformational growth.

With over twenty years of experience in the wellness industry, including more than seventeen years of personal coaching, Kess holds over a dozen certifications and has completed extensive training in physical and mental health. She collaborates with numerous nonprofit organizations across the United States and internationally, equipping people to embrace change, break free from stagnation, and ignite their hearts for the life God intends for them.

Kess is a writer, author, change activation speaker, and transformational life coach. She has led national and international trainings where she shares insights from her professional and personal experiences with pain and trauma. A passionate and dynamic teacher, Kess connects deeply with her audience, grounded in her belief that her love for Jesus is the foundation of her success. She joyfully shares this love with everyone she meets.

Beyond her professional endeavors, Kess is a devoted wife, mother to three grown daughters, and proud "Mimi" to two grandsons. Her mission is to share the love of Jesus and the transformative gifts He offers, helping people move through pain and break the cycle of generational sin. She believes transformation begins with a single step. Are you ready to take yours?

Sanctification is the process of change that comes through a willingness to surrender everything to Jesus while hoping not only to become more like Him but also to exemplify the fruits of the Spirit to those around me as evidence of Christ living in and through me.

Teresa Holbrooks Nichols

Chapter 14

His Plan, His Timing, and Her Willing Heart

By Teresa Holbrooks Nichols

Sanctification is the process of change that comes through a willingness to surrender everything to Jesus while hoping not only to become more like Him but also to exemplify the fruits of the Spirit to those around her as evidence of Christ living in and through her.

"Tell me I'm just having a bad dream," she whispered to herself, knowing this was not the case at all. She found herself totally bewildered by the fact that after being so excited about writing in a new devotional, she now found it so difficult to share her story. She had an overwhelming sense of déjà vu as she glanced at the stacks of pages—proof of her diligence in trying to put words to paper—and realized she'd faced this predicament before. In fact, it was just a year ago that she wrote her first chapter in a cohort publishing project called *More Than Enough: The Silent Struggle of a Woman's Identity*, and she recalled the overwhelming feelings of insecurity that eventually led to her chapter title: "Her Tears Unlocked Her Story."

Even then, she was genuinely shocked at how hard it was to do something she had dreamed of for so long. "Shouldn't it be much easier this time around?" she wondered as frustration crept in. She had witnessed God's faithfulness and watched Him do things she couldn't even imagine with the first book, yet here she was again, struggling with doubt and weighed down by thoughts of her inability to write her story. Honestly, she had even asked what would happen if she pulled out of the project altogether as she faced feelings of utter despair.

Today was a day of reckoning for her. She had submitted a story but knew in her heart she just wasn't satisfied. She reread her words, and while all the ideas were relevant, she knew her main focus had shifted, and her story was not conveying the message she had originally intended. She quickly emailed her editor, asking her to hold off until she got back in touch. She grabbed her computer and began again. . . .

She remembers when she first saw the title *Before She Knew Jesus* and thought this project might not be for her because, frankly, she couldn't remember a time when she didn't know Jesus. Yet, she felt drawn to participate. She could testify that there is a real difference between *knowing about* Jesus and *really knowing* Jesus, and she sensed the importance of sharing actual stories of transformations she had experienced as she had come to know Jesus better. These changes continually shifted her perception of Jesus, even though He always remained the same. From her earliest memories to her present days, Jesus was and is always there!

She knows her story may be a little different than expected, but she's willing to bet that each author will share moments when Jesus changed circumstances and drew them closer. She smiles to herself, knowing she has more to share than one chapter can hold (evidenced by the stacks of stories she'd written), but she is so thankful her focus is back!

She is certain that through this process, Jesus will remind her of exactly who He is *again*. This is necessary because He sees how hard she struggles to *rest* in His forgiveness, mercy, and grace. Rest is something that has never come easy for her. She is guilty of pushing herself to the limit, always trying to accomplish more than one person can possibly achieve, with hopes of somehow earning the love and approval of others, including Jesus. More often than not, she is left feeling as though she has not measured up to their expectations. At those times, she's thankful that Jesus knows her well and never tires of picking her back up out of the dark, messy places where she feels so inadequate, insecure, and undeserving! He always sets her feet back on solid ground!

Still, her mind never stops as it races from one thing to another, refusing to let her sit still for long. She just can't seem to satisfy her inner critic, and the enemy never stops filling her head with haunting feelings of never doing or being enough. Frankly, she's exhausted and knows it is affecting her life in more ways than one. Even her love of writing has seemed wearisome as of late, just another thing on her to-do list, while it once was her way of resting with Jesus, her way of listening and learning.

She is reminded of the story of Martha and Mary in the Bible and ashamedly admits that she sees herself in Martha, the one who is distracted and worried about doing all the "right" things, striving to accomplish things, and completely missing out on the time to rest with Jesus. She wishes she was more like Mary, who stopped everything to spend time with Jesus, sitting at His feet and listening to His words. The Scripture says Martha complained about Mary not helping her, and Jesus replied, "You are worried and upset about many things, but few things are needed—or indeed only one. Mary has chosen what is better, and it will not be taken away from her" (Luke 10:41–42, NIV). This reprimand by Jesus stings a little because she knows that, like Martha, she complains and worries way too often. She whispers a prayer, asking Jesus to help her rest her mind, body, and soul, trusting He's got everything under control.

As she considers her present plight, she feels the need to revisit the past and share where the roots of her faith began, how it's adapted, and how it's still changing. She recalls many areas where insecurity reared its ugly head in her life and lightheartedly cautions her readers to buckle up as she traverses through decades of a life already lived while truly wondering how it all went by so fast. . . .

Many of her earliest memories include her Granny and Papa Chastain, Jesus, and church. One constant in her life was her grandparent's commitment to their faith, each other, and church attendance. Thankfully, they were also determined to take *her* to church, and she would be forever grateful they did. Sunday mornings, Sunday nights, and Wednesday nights were the norm, but she also remembers attending "singings" and "old-time revivals."

Her grandparents loved Jesus and planted the seeds of her faith early on. She loved them dearly, and their bond remained strong throughout the years. The countless memories of hearing them pray and sing are truly precious. Her Papa was perhaps the greatest influence on her desire to follow Jesus. She watched him live out his faith, and he was the one who taught her the importance of prayer. Her memories of him getting down on his knees to pray with her at night were priceless. She fondly recalls him laughing and mimicking the sound of whippoorwills singing in the distance when prayer was over. Other memories include her Papa singing hymns all the way to and from church and how she loved singing in the choir with him. She could almost see herself whispering to him, asking him to request her favorite songs and how he'd give her a sweet, sly smile that made it seem like "their little secret." His love of Jesus helped her love Jesus too, without a doubt!

Some might say she couldn't really have known Jesus at age seven, but she'd be willing to vehemently argue the case! Her tender heart loved and trusted Jesus with things she has never really shared with anyone else to this very day. Jesus was her friend and confidant, and she told Him everything she was afraid to share with others. He knew the hard things, the scary things, and the things she didn't understand. Jesus was her friend . . . before He was her Savior.

The "old country church" they attended was one where most of the congregation knew each other as family or friends. Reverend Davie Wilson was the pastor, and people came from all around to hear him preach. He was a big man who could grip your attention like no other with his firm, strong voice. At times, he'd practically run up and down the aisles as he delivered his sermons. His love of God was evident to all who knew him, and he was greatly respected and loved.

She vividly recalls his sermons about the love and forgiveness of Jesus and how being saved meant that her sins were cast away "as far as the east is from the west" (Psalm 103:12, NIV). That was certainly reassuring! However, other messages included calls for repentance, stern warnings against disobeying God's commandments, and the dangers of backsliding and falling into temptation. All these sermons intertwined, and though she accepted the forgiveness of Jesus, she somehow became fearful that if she didn't live a near-perfect life, she might lose her salvation. She remembers hearing the Scriptures about each person having two roads to choose from. One is narrow and leads to life, and only a few find it; the other is broad and leads to destruction, and many will enter it. As a result, seeds of worry took up residence in her mind and left her fearful of choosing the wrong path.

> *Though she accepted the forgiveness of Jesus, she somehow became fearful that if she didn't live a near-perfect life, she might lose her salvation.*

Honestly, she still combats the enemy's attempts to convince her that she might miss heaven. He consistently tells her she is not enough, and her thoughts take her to painful memories of a broken marriage. She'd married at nineteen and strayed from her faith, believing she was not living a life Jesus would approve of. But she never stopped thinking about Him, even though she ignored feelings of conviction so she could continue "enjoying life" with others—doing things she had been taught were sinful. She found herself divorced seven years later as a result of her spouse's decision to be with someone else, and her feelings of insecurity grew.

During that time, she had to battle memories from her past . . . sermons that seemed to imply hell was the penalty for divorce. These were strong memories for her, as her parents had divorced when she was only seven. She had been so worried because her innocent mind couldn't accept such a fate for the parents she loved so much! So the question became, "Could she date again and possibly remarry, or would that choice separate her from Jesus for eternity?"

Although she leaned on Jesus during this time, she was still not living a life fully committed to Him. She needed answers, and after spending time seeking them (and without going into great detail), her perception of everything shifted. She began to see more clearly what Jesus achieved on her behalf on the cross. *Jesus gave His life to save her from all her sins,* including divorce.

She eventually remarried and gained a sweet little stepdaughter named Carrie. Her married life typically consisted of recreation and entertainment that included drinking or "partying," as they called it in those days. So, once again, this meant that her life did not align with anything she had been taught in church—drunkenness was a sin. She felt convicted, but like before, she did not heed the call.

It wasn't until she became a mother that her desire to return to her faith took center stage in her heart and mind once again. Her life forever changed for the better when God allowed her to become a mother to a beautiful daughter named Kaitlyn. The moment she laid eyes on her baby girl, her heart overflowed with love, and she immediately felt a tug back toward Jesus. Even though she wasn't exactly sure where she stood with her Savior, she found herself praying for Jesus to watch over her baby and keep her safe.

Over the next nine years, God blessed her life with the addition of two more children, a beautiful daughter named Lexie and a precious son named Dylan. She felt the overwhelming magnitude of a mother's love every time she gazed at her children. They were God's gifts to her world, and she was and is forever grateful He chose her to be their mom. Motherhood ignited a desire to share her faith with her children and others, and God softened her heart even more after the decision was made to enroll Kaitlyn at Oconee Christian Academy.

His Plan, His Timing, and Her Willing Heart

Her sweet little girl came home singing songs about Jesus that brought on a flood of memories from her own childhood. Kaitlyn loved to tell her about the things she learned, from Bible stories to prayers and songs. Her momma's heart responded as God knew it would!

A Bible verse came to mind as she looked back at that time in her life. It was one she had chosen as her homeschool verse: "Train up a child in the way he should go, And when he is old he will not depart from it" (Proverbs 22:6, NKJV). She now clearly sees the promise and truth of God's Word, as the training she received from her grandparents and Kaitlyn's sweet faith drew her back to Jesus.

While her girls were still quite young, the Holy Spirit really stirred her heart. One night, she sat on her living room floor, listening to a song her eleven-year-old niece had recorded with her family. She played that song over and over as that sweet voice sang about an everlasting place where there were no tears or pain. The lyrics extended an invitation, asking if she wanted to come along with her to a beautiful place, and she responded, "Yes!" The dam broke, and tears of repentance fell in a flood of raw emotion. In that moment, she chose Jesus again!

Years of pent-up confusion over the logistics of right and wrong and concerns for what she would have to surrender to Jesus had her fearful of what her new commitment to Him might mean. Admittedly, one of the biggest factors weighing on her mind that night was the knowledge that, for her, alcohol would have to go. While the alcohol itself was not something she would miss, she knew, without a doubt, that excluding it would adversely affect some of her closest relationships. Since then, after many years of abstinence she has enjoyed an adult beverage with those she loves, without the intentions of reverting to her old self, but rather to delight and prioritize relationships. Alcohol itself isn't a sin, but the heart's posture toward the drink is the slippery slope that can leave one ensnared in the enemy's trap.

The enemy was really on his game that night, trying hard to dissuade her, bombarding her with fearful thoughts about the opinions of others, and taunting her with the real possibilities of special relationships being severed. She can still recall the internal tug-of-war she experienced. She wanted Jesus's forgiveness but was afraid of change. You can bet she tried bargaining with Jesus on the issue, but she already knew the outcome. *Jesus wanted her to surrender it all to Him, not just some of it.*

> *She can still recall the internal tug-of-war she experienced. She wanted Jesus's forgiveness but was afraid of change.*

She chose Jesus, and she has never looked back! She had strayed, but Jesus never did! He had been walking by her side all along, loving her when she felt unlovable and calling to her in subtle ways through the years, knowing she would return. All those years spent fearing Jesus might leave her were for naught.

As she lets her thoughts drift through the years of memories since she chose Jesus, she feels it's important to confide that it hasn't always been easy to adhere to the convictions of her heart. This has been especially true when her convictions have differed from those of other believers. However, this doesn't make one right and one wrong. Instead, she believes convictions are part of the sanctification process (setting something apart for God's special purpose) and recognizes that purposes are unique and specific convictions might differ from believer to believer. Ultimately, she understands that she must follow the promptings of the Holy Spirit in her life to choose the "right path" for her, even when it's hard. She knows this requires determination and a willingness to stay the course. The enemy knows this is an area where he can stir up chaos and conflict, and he does, hoping she will just give in to fit in. And while she finally realizes that giving into the temptations might not separate her from Jesus, she knows it might hinder her calling to share His Gospel, and that's not something she's willing to chance.

One last story of importance takes her to 2019—when she was experiencing difficult times and really questioning her identity and purpose. She had reached those dreaded middle-age years, with the typical issues that are enough to make anyone question their sanity! But it was more than just that. She knew something important was missing, and after a while, she realized it was *her!*

> *She knew something important was missing, and after a while, she realized it was her!*

Somewhere along the line, she had allowed herself to settle into a routine that required daily balancing acts as she attempted to navigate the obligations that stemmed from the many titles she carried, including, but not limited to, daughter, wife, mother, sister, aunt, friend, author, entrepreneur, and follower of Christ. They each had responsibilities, and together, they kept her busy and frustrated more often than not.

As a result, she forgot who she was before the titles. Who was Teresa before life happened? She still had her faith but felt ineffective for Christ. The search to discover her true identity sparked a desire to seek God's purpose for her life, ultimately revealing a dream she had almost given up on. Oh, how she'd imagined that her love of writing and journaling might one day result in her holding an actual book that she had written and published in her hands!

Ideas for how she could start writing and sharing the gospel on social media sprung to life. She took a leap of faith, and after much debate, her daughter helped her create a name for the pages she would post on social media: Uniquely Constructed on Facebook and Uniquelyconstucted67 on Instagram. In her mind, the two words seemed to work together. *She could picture God constructing the pieces of her calling, layer upon layer, removing the imperfections and creating the paths that would lead her toward becoming the woman He wanted her to be.* God created her uniquely, and construction was the business industry she worked in; thus, Uniquely Constructed was birthed. Perfect!

With the decision to share the Gospel came a deliberate commitment to carve out time to write, study, and learn, all to bring her dream to life. She was all in! For the first time in a long time, she felt like she was moving in the right direction. And, with a little patience, she finally saw God opening doors of opportunity. With His divine connections, she now writes a column (also called "Uniquely Constructed") for a website called Patheos on their Evangelical Channel, and she has a published chapter in a book she can hold in her hands titled *More Than Enough: The Silent Struggle of a Woman's Identity*.

Can you see the irony of that title? God certainly has a sense of humor! If you'd asked her a few years ago whether she'd ever write about being "more than enough," she would have emphatically and laughingly replied, "Absolutely Not!" Yet, that's exactly what God opened the doors for her to do. She never could have guessed what the intertwining of His plan, His timing, and her willing heart would lead to. She pauses and gives God praise; His faithfulness and provision overwhelm her!

In closing, she wants to share some thoughts from her journal about who Jesus is to her now:

> *This Jesus she knows is so simple on the one hand ~ yet so complex on the other.*

> *He's a friend one minute, encouraging and cheering her on ~ and a Savior the next, extending His hands of mercy and grace to cover her mistakes.*

> *He's a listener to the petitions of her heart ~ and a wonderful companion she turns to when her heart is broken.*

> *He's caring and compassionate when she yearns to feel loved ~ yet stern and unyielding when reminding her to be about her Father's business.*

He's the one who will speak to the Father on her behalf when she's sinned and fallen short ~ yet will remind her to listen to the Holy Spirit's conviction when she needs to change.

He's the one who loves her unconditionally, even as she feels so undeserving ~ and He's the one who patiently reminds her that she doesn't have to earn His love because He chose to give it to her freely.

Jesus is ALL she's ever needed ~ this Jesus is her everything.

What areas of your life have shifted your perception of who Jesus was and who He is to you now, and were there times when you thought He'd abandoned you but later realized He had been faithfully by your side through every step?

pray

Reflect

Write

TERESA HOLBROOKS NICHOLS is a woman on a mission to "Go and Tell The World About Jesus!" She holds many titles, including, but not limited to, daughter, wife, mother, sister, aunt, friend, author, licensed residential builder, general contractor, real estate agent, and, most importantly, follower of Christ. Raising a family, homeschooling children, and owning and operating a construction business required much of her focus for many years. She often felt she was called to do more and struggled with feelings that told her something was missing. Finally, God assured her she was on the right path. He reminded her that her first mission field was her home, teaching her children about Jesus, and that He would later extend her mission field outward.

Teresa can testify to His faithfulness as she now walks into new opportunities to share her story, hoping to help others find and follow Jesus. She excitedly became a published author contributor to *More Than Enough: The Silent Struggle of a Woman's Identity* alongside an amazing group of women she now calls friends. She is the creator of Uniquely Constructed and writes a column by that name for the Patheos Evangelical Channel and Facebook. She can also be found on Instagram at Uniquelyconstructed67.

Teresa knows God is propelling her forward and anxiously seeks to become exactly who God uniquely created her to be while achieving all He has for her to do! She has added the titles of "Gammy" and "Nanny" to her resume in recent years and enjoys every minute she spends with her grandbabies. She loves spending time with her family and continuously reminds them of her love by saying, "I love you more than words can say, always and forever!"

Sanctification is shedding the world and its influences and taking a hard right turn onto the narrow road.

Candice Brown

Chapter 15

Awakening to Truth: Choosing the Narrow Path over Deception

By Candice Brown

*S*anctification is shedding the world and its influences and taking a hard right turn onto the narrow road.

A beautiful sister in Christ once told me I am a dynamic part of Christ. It wasn't until I started writing this chapter that I understood what she meant. When describing a person, the definition of *dynamic* is someone lively, energetic, impactful, and forceful. This introductory disclaimer, per se, was entered after the chapter was completed. I didn't know the Holy Spirit would lead me on a path to write a warning. This chapter isn't about grace. We have become so grace-oriented that it isn't even biblical. This is about the Truth. The Lord says whoever endures to the end will be saved. Whatever sins you are doing willfully are beyond salvation (Hebrews 10:26) and must be crushed by your heel. If Paul were here today, how many letters would he write? How many warnings would he issue? The Corinthian Church had been baptized, yet Paul still urged them to examine their faith. Even after years of learning, he reminded them to return to the very foundations of His teachings. So this is a warning letter—the lively, impactful, energetic, yet forceful part of Christ.

> *This chapter isn't about grace. We have become so grace-oriented that it isn't even biblical.*

Before I knew Jesus, I was deceived. At thirteen, I raised my hand within the four walls of a church, went to the altar, and said the prayer. "I'm saved?! Of course, I believe Jesus died on the cross for my sins. Of course, I know God sent Him to save us. Now I'm going to heaven? That's it? That was easy!" What a deception that was. I walked away that day—and for twenty-five years after—with no understanding of who Jesus actually was, why He had to fulfill every Old Testament sacrifice with His body, how I was to serve Him, or what it meant to be the salt of the earth. I believed going to the altar and saying the prayer were enough. I was under the illusion of my salvation. As such, under the veil of the enemy's deception, the Church has taken this false sense of assurance theology and presented it as truth to "believers." When God brings His people home, many who believe in Jesus will be left completely confused as to why they aren't in their mansions in heaven—while Jesus's followers, rooting their foundation in Christ, suffering in His name, and blessed with the fruits of the Spirit, will be with the Father and the Son.

What woke me up? It was a bullet to my pride meant to take my life, shaking me to my core—a complete degradation of a dream I would have killed for and the one idol I cared about most: my career. That idol led me away from the foundational teachings of the Bible, creating pervasive addictions that only I knew about for a decade. Willful sins grew from subtle to insidious, opening doors to demonic influences and compromising my salvation. My entire life was infiltrated by that idol, shaping my thoughts and behavior; I had succumbed to the world that Satan is the ruler of (John 12:31).

But that bullet profoundly changed my life. It was Him, bringing back His stray, giving me my life back (Ezekiel 34:16). At that moment, I quite literally woke up. I awoke from my slumber, realizing I no longer had convictions. False information and denying the truth became evident. I had succumbed to not only idolizing my career, where I was working ungodly hours, dreaming of titles and money, and relishing in prideful behavior, but I was also engaged in premarital sex, drunkenness, drug addiction, gossiping, lying, foul language, secular music, secular television, secular books, pagan holidays, and standing for values that didn't align with the Bible (if they were values at all). These things had consumed my life. When I woke up, I couldn't believe who I had become. Shame filled my soul. But because that bullet hit me with a purpose, I didn't sit in shame for long. I started to shed those strongholds one by one. Some took longer than others, and one required that I be delivered from a demon. But through the sanctification process, I began shedding the world and receiving daily revelations from the Holy Spirit.

I grew up in a Christian home, was active in church, participated in the Fellowship of Christian Athletes, and graduated from a Christian university. I thought I "knew" who Jesus was, but I had a superficial understanding of the Gospel. Just because Christians go to church or surround themselves with other Christians doesn't mean they are pursuing righteousness or are on the narrow road. Like that thirteen-year-old girl who raised her hand, went to the altar, and said the prayer, they are just participating in religious activities that lure people into the deception that they will be anxiously awaited by Jesus at the gates. That was me—under two deceptions the church has proclaimed as Truth.

My life was about me. My prayers were about what God could do for me— how He could help my family, how He could get me the title I worked so hard for, and how He could give me more money and the desires of my heart. And, often, my prayers asked, "Why is this happening to me?"—all while being in deep, willful sin. Give me, give me, why, why . . . that is not what we are made for. Our entire existence should be about Him, worshipping and praising Him in everything we do. Our prayers should be about seeking wisdom on how we can serve Him in this world. It isn't about me, you, or the next person. It's about Him—period.

I was on the broad road leading to the wide gate of destruction (Matthew 7:13–14). But after taking that hard right turn onto the narrow road, I learned that you must embrace a new mindset and eliminate the old. Hell is constantly looking back. Fear, anxiety, and shame over what you did or what you should have done is Hell. This is why God says not to look back—this is what Hell is. There are 170 women mentioned by name in the Bible, and Jesus only tells us to remember one: Lot's wife. While delivering her family out of sin so widespread that He destroyed an entire city, God told her never to look back. If we, like her, look back instead of spreading our salt on the earth, we will become pillars of salt, stuck. Sanctification is not looking back; do not get stuck in the past. You must stay steady on the narrow road.

Sanctification is a lifelong journey. You never get off the road. No one is righteous. Christ was tortured beyond recognition, and none of us deserve the sacrifice of His blood. But through cleansing, purifying, and pruning, conviction comes to the hearts of Holy Spirit-filled followers. When I awoke from my secular lifestyle and removed the devil's beguiling veil of confusion, my first conviction was my idol. It took nine months, but ultimately, through strength and obedience (even though there was peace without understanding), I walked away from my career and never looked back. By never looking back, my lack of conviction in other areas of my life started to surface. Sex was next, followed by the release of a drug addiction, which had given the enemy full control over me.

By turning onto the narrow road, my convictions flooded in. So much so that once the Holy Spirit convicted me, I cut out the unholy practices immediately, including the drug use. If you have lost your convictions, you should take hold of every part of your life and mind and seek repentance. When traveling down the wrong road, God will confront you in your sin, and you are to go with Him. Don't be blind to your sin. Listen when the conviction comes. Repent and do not willfully walk in that sin again.

Take a hard right turn onto the narrow road now. Do not arrive at the small gate and have Jesus tell you He doesn't know you. Do not believe what the world tells you. Believing in Jesus isn't the Truth. Knowing Him, serving Him, and keeping your eyes only on Him is the Way. In Luke 13:5, Jesus told His followers they would never make it into the kingdom of heaven unless they repented. They followed Him. They were with Him every day, yet they still didn't understand sanctification. Oh, how many will be the same? How many will spend their lives believing they knew Him, doing their "best" and being a good person, but never fully understanding it is the hard right turn onto the narrow road that leads to the small gate?

The wide road symbolizes our contemporary culture, evidenced by self-dependence and self-absorption—an attitude of "me, me, me." All religions outside Christianity teach that if you are "good enough" and follow their rules and practices, you might earn your way to eternal life. Those are false teachings, apostates prowling around like lions. The Church is altering its beliefs to be more appealing and relevant to contemporary society. A true relationship with Christ is about growth, discipline, and sacrifice. You can't go down both roads at the same time. Your legs will start to straddle them, and you will eventually have to pick a side.

For me, having a genuine relationship with Christ is about understanding the Word. This has been part of my sanctification process. I had been deceived for so long about what the Bible actually says; I now research every word and discern the revelations through the Holy Spirit. Every verse explodes on me, opening new avenues of understanding that have expanded my worship. You need to understand the times of the Bible. Every word was written for a reason. Nothing is without a purpose. Read each word slowly. Look up words, places, and names you aren't familiar with. Every single word in the Bible is written to show us His power. It shows us why Jesus had to come, which is revealed in every verse of the Old Testament. It shows us that the New Testament is the same book as the Old Testament. It shows us how corrupt the world is and how to overcome it. If you understand the times of the Bible, God's Word will show you what to do in our modern times.

In the ancient Middle East, if you loved salt or sold it as a product, you would go to the Dead Sea shore and gather it with the sand. At times, when you returned home, you might notice that too much sand had joined with the salt. As a result, the salt and sand mixture would be thrown into the streets; this is what they did with their rubbish. In Matthew 5:13, Jesus spoke about salt being thrown out into the streets when it lost its flavor. He was speaking to the people in plain language so they would understand the ultimate meaning of His sermon. Be the salt. Don't lose your flavor by mixing with the ways of the world. When you look at sodium chloride, it can only lose its flavor or "worth" if mixed with other substances. It doesn't cease being salt, but it loses its quality.

Jesus says we are the salt of the earth (Matthew 5:13), but we lose our saltiness by mixing in with worldly secularism. And when we are surrounded by too much of that worldly societal pull, we feel pressured to conform while trying to demonstrate our credibility and similarity to a contemporary generation. Jesus says salt will be trampled on if it loses its flavor. If we, His followers, conform to the ways of the world, we, too, will be treated with disgust and looked at with contempt by non-Christians. You can see this in the world today. Believers who mix in with the world lose their saltiness and are viewed with disdain by unbelievers. Jesus also asks us, "But if the salt loses its saltiness, how can it be made salty again?" (Matthew 5:13, NIV). This is a warning. Once your salt loses its saltiness, you can't get it back, and once you lose your reputation with unbelievers, you can't regain it. You become useless salt. We are only salt if we maintain our differences from the world around us.

> *We are only salt if we maintain our differences from the world around us.*

God's design for us and His earth is directly aligned with Christ's message about being the salt. Without enough salt in our bodies, we will experience nausea, vomiting, headaches, confusion, loss of energy, fatigue, restlessness, irritability, and muscle weakness. If the oceans lose their salt, it would be a cataclysmic event. There would be earthquakes everywhere, and volcanoes would erupt in every corner of the earth. What happens to soil if you add a little salt? It improves the soil by producing better water and oxygen flow to plants. The point is this: Christ told us we are the salt because it is an essential part of God's design. Without God's salt, lost souls wouldn't find Christ.

Satan doesn't care if you go to church and "get saved" the way I did. He doesn't care if you continue to go and listen to the fluff or false doctrine of the Western Church. He doesn't care if you wear a cross around your neck. He doesn't care if you have a nativity scene on your lawn during Christmas. He doesn't care if you go to Bible study. He doesn't care about your religious activity. He will let you practice the many religious beliefs that stem from his pagan rituals, created thousands of years ago by his children. As long as you are not walking out your sanctification with Christ or making a continuous effort to discern what is truly holy and righteous, you have no smell to him. You aren't salt—the aroma that is pleasing to God.

We are told to hate what God hates and love what He loves (Psalm 97:10). This verse directly tells us to detest what opposes God's nature. The world may offer its way, but we won't find what we truly need in the kingdom of God if we remain anchored to the world. The god of this age (2 Corinthians 4:4) ensures that any opposition to his ways is no longer met with just criticism but with persecution as well. This shouldn't be a surprise to us. We know we will be persecuted if we don't conform to the world. We will suffer for Him. There is no way around it if you are truly in a relationship with Christ. You must show up for Him. The unholy practices belonging to this world are not allowed on the road to life. This is Satan's work. He has confused the sanctification process, which leads to eternal life, and believers have been deceived.

> *You must show up for Him.*

The narrow road represents standing strong for Christ, a challenging yet righteous path blessed by God. *God is faithful.* He is faithful in the delays. He is faithful in the sin that only He knows. And He is faithful as we walk into the unknown. He longs for us to know the power and presence of what is faith. What looks like an ending has the full capability to become God's new beginning. Whatever you are chasing after, it would chase you if you put God first. I am evidence of this. Jesus is the small gate at the end of the narrow road. Be one of the few who will find it.

"If the world hates you, know that it hated Me before you. If you were of the world, the world would love his own. But because you are not of the world, but I have chosen you out of the world, therefore the world hates you" (John 15:18–19, RGT).

It is confirmed that you are a faithful minister of Christ, when you are hated by the world that hated our King (paraphrased footnote of the 1599 Geneva Bible, John 15: 18–19).

Is the cross a crutch? Do you willfully sin, believing you can return to the cross each time and receive grace?

pray

Reflect

CANDICE BROWN. Wife to a patient man who trusts God's plan. Mother to a giant slayer. Biblical erudite. Kingdom Teacher.

Appendix

Page 8. Through *sanctification*, the surrendering of our lives to Christ, we are accepted, made right in God's eyes, and no longer apart from Him—we are set apart. —**Victoria Ciresi**

Page 20. The transformation from our sinful human nature into a *sanctified* (holy) being is a beautiful thing, but it is often a messy process. Like a cocoon releasing a butterfly, we evolve from our old nature into something spectacular. This process is only achieved with the help of God himself but requires our cooperation. —**Jenny Ingels**

Page 32. *Sanctification* is the process of God guiding us to maturity by renewing our minds, hearts, and desires for the purpose of displaying Christ to the world. —**Jennifer Beeman**

Page 42. *Sanctification* is the ongoing recognition of our desperate need for a Savior to rescue us from ourselves. It is the journey of transformation where God uses our struggles and brokenness to refine us, drawing us closer to Him. It is the process of learning to depend on God's grace in every moment, recognizing that our worth and identity are not rooted in our performance but in His unchanging love. —**Kali Dunson**

Page 56. *Sanctification* is the lifelong process of *knowing* God and being transformed by the *knowing* of God. —**Rebecca "Becky" Vasquez**

Page 66. *Sanctification*, becoming like Jesus and being known by Jesus, isn't a one-off encounter or a good Sunday sermon. It's the leaning in when nothing makes sense in order to sense His existence in the void of senses. —**Tamra Andress**

Page 78. *Sanctification* is the process of removing impurities from an object or person. Unlike purification, it is not a one-time thing but a continual renewing or removal of impurities that occur over time. Sanctification is a gradual deepening of our understanding of Christ and the power we have access to because of who He is, not who we are. —**Jori O'Neale**

Page 88. *Sanctification* is an exciting adventure with Jesus—a daily invitation to take hold of His hand and, with steps of faith, become the amazing person your heavenly Father created you to be. This process is full of ups and downs, twists and turns, and mountain tops and valleys. Sometimes, it is both exciting and scary, as the details aren't always made clear. Yet, one powerful truth always remains the same: Jesus is always present, always faithful, and always victorious. —**Ashley Weston**

Page 98. "When I pray, 'Lord, show me what sanctification means for me', He will show me. It means being made one with Jesus. Sanctification is not something Jesus puts in me—it is Himself in me (1 Corinthians 1:30)." —Oswald Chambers, My Utmost for His Highest (emphasis added) —**April Foster**

Page 110. Allowing the Holy Spirit complete autonomy involves surrendering to His work in order to remove everything that is not reflective of Christ. This process of *sanctification* purifies our minds and souls, requiring us to submit to His transformative power and actively engage in the crucifixion of lies and beliefs that have kept us enslaved to darkness—ultimately leading to spiritual freedom and alignment with God's truth. —**Amber Love**

Page 122. *Sanctification* is the ongoing journey after coming to faith through which we are gradually transformed to reflect the character, values, and behavior that align more closely with a holy and moral life. It's like growing spiritually, where old, harmful habits and mindsets are slowly replaced by virtues and a deeper relationship with Christ. —**Christina Blincoe**

Page 136. *Sanctification* is the lifelong process of becoming less like ourselves and more like Jesus. —**Heather Demorest**

Appendix

Page 148. *Sanctification* is like God giving me a new gift each day, inviting me to open it, use it, and be in awe of His provision while wrestling with my pride, wanting to do it myself, and seeking praise. It's a daily process of learning to surrender and trusting that His gift is what truly transforms me, even when I resist like a child. —**Kess Scharff**

Page 162. *Sanctification* is the process of change that comes through a willingness to surrender everything to Jesus while hoping not only to become more like Him but also to exemplify the fruits of the Spirit to those around me as evidence of Christ living in and through me. —**Teresa Holbrooks Nichols**

Page 178. *Sanctification* is shedding the world and its influences and taking a hard right turn onto the narrow road. —**Candice Brown**

Acknowledgments

This project wouldn't be in existence without the creative and diligent minds behind the F.I.T. In Faith Press team. To Candice, who brought the concept to the table, thoroughly prayed for and selected each author, and meticulously prepared it for publishing. To Becky, for her brilliant gift of bringing life to the idea and designs for the cover and marketing. To Sharon, for pressing into every word and supporting each woman as they revealed the layers of themselves they have always held sacred. To Kali, for helping move the mission socially. And to the community of authors who spent months with the Lord as they submitted their pride and plans to His perfect will through their stories and for this message. During a season of personal and even deeper sanctification, I'm humbled beyond measure to have my name alongside yours in this book and, more importantly, to call you sisters in Christ.

F. I.T. PRESS

Your story doesn't just matter for you, it matters to move others!

1 CHRONICLES 16:24 (NLT)
*Publish His glorious deeds among the nations.
Tell everyone about the amazing things he does.*

A Christian Publishing House dedicated to turning messages into movements. On mission to mobilize the critical voices for such a time as this. Specializing in co-hort compilations, to make way for writers to collaborate with other prolific members of the Body of Christ. Our works open conversations around mental, physical, relational, financial and spiritual health and wholeness journeys, often directly associated to our rooted identity and purpose driven life.

Learn More & Don't Wait to Get Published!

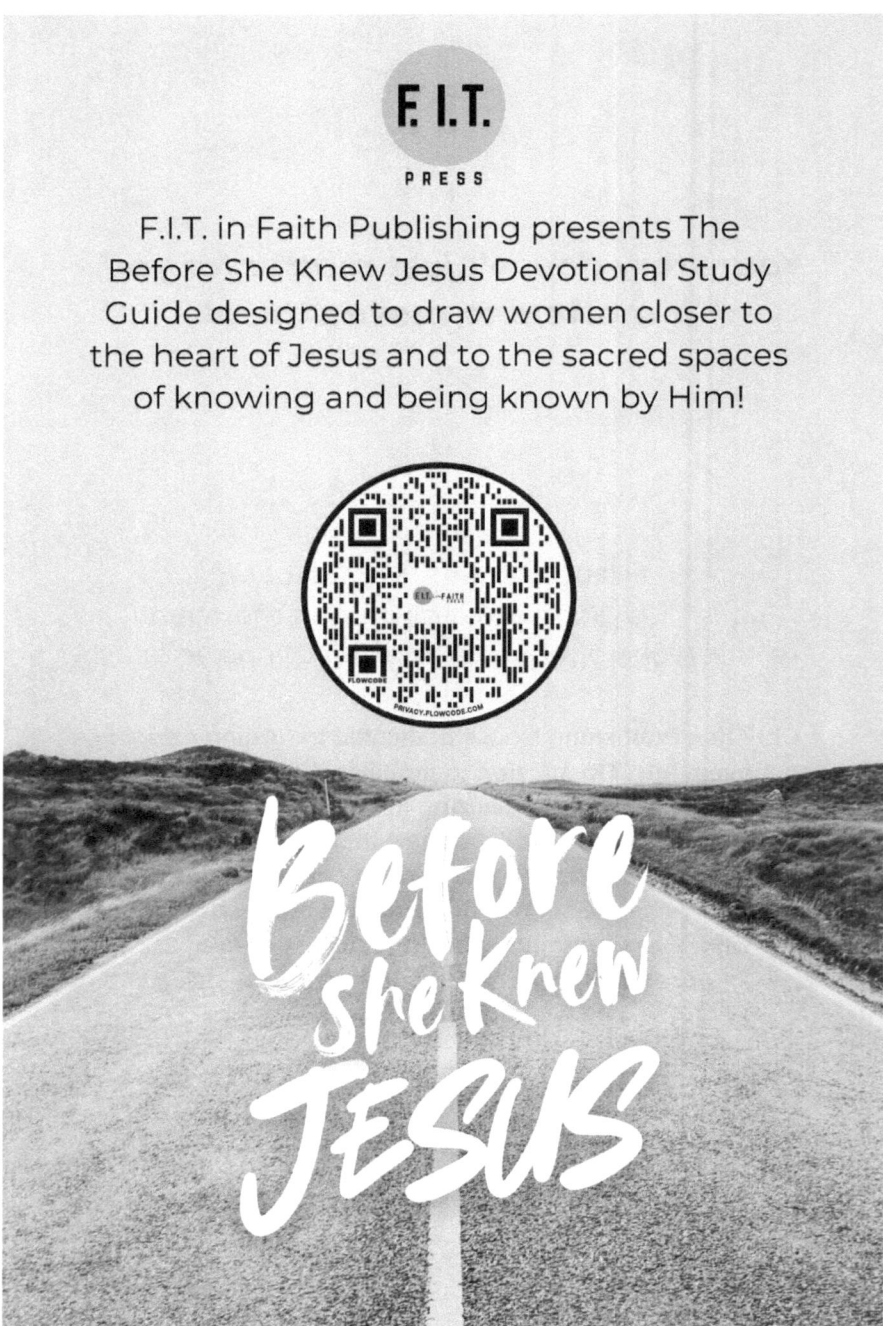

Join us on a devotional journey to
Finding Joy in God AND Breaking Out of the Boxes the World Puts Us In!
F.I.T. Press presents *More Than Enough: The Silent Struggle of a Women's Identity*

You are more than...
More than a Religion
More Than a Mom
More than a Wife
More than My Past
More than my body
More than my job

Get the More Than Enough Devotional Companion Study Guide : A 38 page biblical resource + 9 videos www.fitinfaithmedia.com/devotional

Before she Knew JESUS

Ladies! Beauty Awaits from the inside-out and outside-in.

We will explore every detail of God's wondrous creation. Starting with YOU! This wellness retreat is an immersive experience intended to get you back to the basics (mind, body, and HOLY spirit) by heightening your senses to what matters most: your vertical alignment, so you can horizontally serve, share, and SHINE!

Fella's! The Great Outdoor Awaits! Embark. Elevate. Expand. Explore.

Getting primal to perform at our highest potential as men, husbands, fathers, and leaders by activating our sonship. Join us on this "unforgettable, epic, and life-changing" adventure that will catalyze you to exist in your power, authority, and passion.

Contact: hello@thefoundercollective.org

HAVE YOU EVER WONDERED?

What your purpose is?

How you could use your giftings as a global messenger for God?

How your spiritual gifts are connected to your prosperity?

How your passion propels your profit?

This is a podcast for the messengers!
The called ones.
The mobilized ones.
The ones on a mission to turn their message into a movement.

This show was designed for Declaring Truth, Transforming Narratives & *Catalyzing Christians* to Speak, Write, Build & Testify.

SUBSCRIBE & LEAVE A REVIEW FOR A SHOUTOUT ON AIR!

JOIN THE F.I.T. in Faith Network Resource Hub!

IT'S TIME TO ACTIVATE YOUR *god dream*

DOWNLOAD NOW!

The F.I.T. in Faith Network Resource Hub will serve as a growth tool for you as a Fierce Female ready to Fight The Good Fight.

SPEAK, WRITE, BUILD, TESTIFY

Count this app as your Aaron and Hurr on your fulfilling and sometimes hard days of blazing the trail of your purpose-driven calling.

- **SOUND BIBLICAL BUSINESS SUPPORT - COURSES & CONTENT**
- **TRAINING & IMPLEMENTATION TOOLS**
- **TEMPLATES**
- **QUICK START RESOURCES**
- **FINANCIAL TRAJECTORY PLANS & MODELS**
- **COMMUNITY CONNECTIONS - FOCUS GROUPS**
- **LIVE OFFICE HOURS MONTHLY WITH Q&A AND ON THE SPOT COACHING**

This is a movement of empowered legacy building, chain breaking, pioneers, liberating others to stand in freedom, firm in their identity, and activating authority as Kingdom citizens. Join the movement today.

WE ARE THE MOBILIZED CHURCH!

www.ingramcontent.com/pod-product-compliance
Lightning Source LLC
Chambersburg PA
CBHW060601080526
44585CB00013B/647